Stoic Principles Reimagined

Also from EATMS Productions

Books on power, survival, women's autonomy, and the systems shaping modern America.

Nonfiction

Billionaires, Capitalism, and Power

Evil and the Mountain Ungreed
Self Help for American Billionaires
Selfish Steve and the Ivory Tower
Tariffs, Taxes, & Face-Eating Leopards
Ban Billionaires: Fascism Fix

Fascism, Religion, and Cultural Control

Self Help for the Manosphere
Fascism 2025
Fascism & the Perverts & the Greed Virus
Christian Fascism Marriage Book
Tyranny, Table Manners, & Tiramisu

Guides for Women's Autonomy and Protection

How to Survive in Post-America as a Woman
Project 2025 American Drag
4B – Burn, Ban, Boycott, Build
4B OG – So No Go GYN
I'm Glad He's Dead

Analysis of Authoritarian Project 2025

Project 2025: The Blueprint
Project 2025: The List
Project 2025, Christian Dumb Dumbs, & The Republican Agenda
Fascism, Project 2025, & The Pinkprint

Modern Rewrites for Women

Stoic Principles Reimagined
Siddhartha Reimagined
The Prince Reimagined for Women
The Art of War Reimagined for Women
The Jungle Reimagined
The Constitution Reimagined for Women

Machine Learning Series

AI, Bitcoin, Nostr for Women
AI, Safety, & Security for Women
AI, Anxiety, & Health for Women
AI, Kids, & Family Safety for Women
AI, Creativity, & Personal Expression for Women
AI, Independent Work, & Parallel Power for Women

Social Systems Series

Emotional Labor for Women
Household Power for Women
Workplace Power for Women
Medical Bias for Women
Aging Systems for Women
Recovery Systems for Women

Fiction

Dystopian Stories of Resistance and Collapse

Propaganda Paige & the Missing Prosperity
Propaganda Paige & the TIDE Manifesto
Propaganda Paige & the Shadow Cartographers
Propaganda Paige & the Prosperity Alliance
Propaganda Paige & the Shattered Truth
Propaganda Paige & the Rising TIDE
Propaganda Paige & the Last Bastion
Propaganda Paige & the Dawn of Prosperity
Project 2025: Dorian — The Last Men
Project 2025: Boy — A Last Men Novel

Stoic Principles Reimagined For Modern Challenges

by
Esme Mees

E A T M S
P R O D U C T I O N S

ISBN: 978-1-966014-96-6

Cover, interior design, interior prints by: Esme Mees

eatms@pm.me
www.eatms.me

Printed in the United States of America.

Imagination is the beginning of creation.

—George Bernard Shaw

Table of Contents

Unremarkable 1, 2024

Introduction

Beginning the Conversation

Imagine standing on the edge of a vast, ancient library, where the wisdom of the ages is stored in rows upon rows of dusty old books. The air is thick with the scent of parchment, and the faint whispers of long-dead philosophers seem to linger in the air. Among these books is Meditations by Marcus Aurelius, a collection of reflections written nearly two thousand years ago by a Roman emperor who ruled during a time of great turmoil. It's the kind of book that feels distant, almost unreachable, as if its wisdom belongs to another era entirely—an era where the concerns of emperors were far removed from the challenges we face today.

But what if I told you that buried within those ancient pages is a blueprint for navigating the very struggles that define our modern world? What if the thoughts of a Roman emperor could help us make sense of the chaos and injustice that swirl around us today? It might seem improbable, but sometimes the most profound insights come from the most unexpected places. Take a moment to consider the world we live in now. It's a world where the forces of patriarchy, bigotry, and unchecked capitalism seem more entrenched than ever—where inequality runs deep, the planet teeters on the brink of environmental catastrophe, and entire communities are marginalized and silenced. It's easy to feel overwhelmed, to wonder how we can possibly make a difference in the face of such overwhelming odds. *Stoic Principles Reimagined for Modern Challenges* seeks to calm our frazzled minds by revisiting a great stoic mind of the past.

Yet, in this very moment, as we grapple with these challenges, there's something powerful about turning to ancient wisdom—not to escape the present, but to reimagine it. Marcus Aurelius wrote Meditations as a way to understand himself and his place in the world, to cultivate a sense of inner peace and virtue amidst the storms of life. But what if we took his reflections and viewed them through a different lens? What if we reinterpreted his Stoic philosophy to not only address our personal struggles but also to confront the systemic injustices that plague our society?

Let's think about it. Marcus Aurelius was a man of immense power, a ruler who had to navigate the complexities of an empire in crisis. Yet, his writings are intensely personal, focused on the inner life, on how to live with integrity in a world that often feels out of control. He urges himself to remain calm, to accept what he cannot change, to be virtuous in the face of adversity. These are timeless principles, but they take on a new dimension when we consider them in light of today's challenges. In our world, where so much of life is shaped by forces beyond our control, whether it's the economy, climate change, or the pervasive structures of inequality, Marcus's emphasis on personal responsibility can feel almost inadequate. Yes, it's important to cultivate inner strength and resilience, but is that enough? Is it enough to focus on our own virtue when the world around us is in turmoil?

This is where the reimagining begins. What if we expanded Marcus's Stoic principles to include not just personal responsibility, but also social accountability? What if, instead of simply accepting the world as it is, we used his teachings to actively engage with it, to challenge the systems that perpetuate injustice, and to work toward a more equitable and compassionate society? The idea might sound radical, but it's also deeply necessary. We are living in a time where the old ways of thinking, rooted in individualism and isolation—are no longer sufficient. The problems we face are collective, and so too must be our solutions. By reinterpreting *Meditations* through a progressive lens, we can find new ways to navigate the complexities of our world, ways that honor both our personal integrity and our collective responsibility.

Context and Background

To truly grasp the significance of reimagining *Meditations* by Marcus Aurelius, it's essential to understand the world in which it was written, as well as the world we're living in now. The distance between the two might seem vast at first glance—after all, we're talking about a Roman emperor who ruled almost two millennia ago. But when you dig deeper, you begin to see the threads that connect the past to the present, the timelessness of certain human struggles, and the ways in which ancient wisdom can be adapted to meet the challenges of our time.

Let's start with Marcus Aurelius himself. Born in 121 CE, Marcus was groomed for leadership from an early age. By the time he ascended to the throne as Roman Emperor in 161 CE, the empire was at a pivotal moment, facing internal strife, external threats, and the constant pressure of managing vast territories and diverse populations. As emperor, Marcus was responsible for maintaining the stability of an empire that spanned three continents, a task that required not only military and political acumen but also an extraordinary degree of personal fortitude. It was during these years of leadership, amidst the chaos of wars and political machinations, that Marcus wrote Meditations. Unlike many other philosophical works of the time, Meditations wasn't intended for public consumption. These writings were personal reflections, a kind of philosophical diary, where Marcus sought to make sense of his life, his responsibilities, and the broader world. The text is steeped in Stoic philosophy, a school of thought that emphasizes rationality, self-control, and the acceptance of fate.

Stoicism, as Marcus Aurelius practiced it, was about maintaining one's integrity and inner peace regardless of external circumstances. The Stoics believed that while we can't control what happens to us, we can control how we respond. For Marcus, this meant constantly reminding himself to act with virtue, to remain calm in the face of adversity, and to accept the natural order of things.

But as we bring Marcus's ideas into the present day, it's crucial to recognize the context in which he wrote. Marcus Aurelius was a man of immense power, a ruler whose decisions affected millions. His reflections are those of someone who operated from a position of privilege, whose concerns, while deeply personal, were also shaped by the responsibilities and realities of leading an empire. This context is important because it highlights both the strengths and limitations of his philosophy when applied to the broader population, particularly those who do not hold power.

Fast forward to today, and the world looks very different on the surface. We're no longer living in a sprawling Roman Empire, but in a globalized society marked by rapid technological advancements, unprecedented levels of interconnectedness, and equally unprecedented challenges. Yet, in many ways, the core issues that Marcus Aurelius grappled with, power, responsibility, virtue, and the quest for inner peace, remain deeply relevant.

However, our contemporary context adds layers of complexity to these issues. The challenges we face today are both personal and systemic, with social, political, and environmental crises that require us to rethink not just how we live as individuals, but how we live as a collective. In many parts of the world, patriarchy, bigotry, and capitalism continue to shape the structures of power and privilege, often to the detriment of marginalized communities. Inequality is deeply entrenched, with the gap between the wealthy and the poor widening year after year. Climate change threatens the very survival of our planet, demanding urgent action and a fundamental shift in how we interact with the natural world.

In this context, the traditional Stoic emphasis on personal responsibility, while valuable, can seem insufficient. It's not enough to focus solely on cultivating inner peace and virtue

14

when the world around us is on fire—both literally and figuratively. What's needed is a philosophy that not only helps us navigate our own lives but also empowers us to engage with and change the world for the better. This is where the reimagining of *Meditations* comes into play. By taking the foundational principles of Stoicism, self-discipline, rationality, acceptance, and expanding them to include a broader social and environmental consciousness, we can create a more holistic approach to living a good life. One that recognizes the interconnectedness of all things and the importance of addressing systemic injustices as part of our pursuit of virtue.

This reimagining is not about discarding the wisdom of Marcus Aurelius, but rather about building on it, adapting it to the needs and realities of the 21st century. It's about taking those timeless reflections on how to live with integrity and applying them to the urgent tasks of dismantling oppressive systems, building equitable communities, and caring for our planet. As we embark on this exploration of *Meditations* through a progressive lens, it's important to keep in mind both the historical context of Marcus's writings and the contemporary context in which we find ourselves. By doing so, we can bridge the gap between the past and the present, drawing on the wisdom of the ancients to inform our actions today, and perhaps, to carve out a better future.

In the pages that follow, we'll delve deeper into how Marcus's Stoic philosophy can be reinterpreted to address modern challenges, from personal growth to social justice, from inner peace to collective responsibility. By understanding the context and background of both the original text and our current world, we can begin to see how ancient wisdom can serve as a guide for progressive change, helping us to navigate the complexities of our time with clarity, purpose, and a commitment to making a difference.

Purpose of the Book

At first glance, the idea of revisiting an ancient text like Meditations by Marcus Aurelius might seem like an exercise in nostalgia, a way to connect with the past, perhaps, or to find solace in timeless wisdom. But this book isn't just about looking backward. Instead, it's about taking the profound insights of a long-dead emperor and reinterpreting them in a way that speaks directly to the urgent needs of our time.

So why reimagine Meditations now, in the 21st century? The answer lies in the profound challenges we face today, challenges that require not only individual resilience but also collective action. We live in a world where systemic injustices, environmental degradation, and deepening social divisions threaten the fabric of our societies. The traditional Stoic focus on personal virtue and inner peace, while invaluable, must be expanded to include a broader social consciousness that addresses these pressing issues. The purpose of this book is to bridge the gap between the personal and the political, between ancient wisdom and modern reality. By reinterpreting Meditations through a progressive lens, this book aims to offer a new kind of philosophy, one that not only helps individuals navigate their personal struggles but also empowers them to engage with and transform the world around them.

This reimagining is not about replacing the original teachings of Marcus Aurelius, but about building upon them, adapting them to meet the challenges of our time. It's about recognizing that the pursuit of virtue cannot be separated from the pursuit of justice, and that true inner peace is impossible without addressing the systemic injustices that affect us all. In a world where the forces of patriarchy, bigotry, and unchecked capitalism continue to perpetuate inequality and suffering, this book seeks to offer a framework for living that is both personally fulfilling and socially responsible. It challenges the reader to rethink what it means to live a good life in the modern world, one that is not only centered on self-discipline and inner tranquility but also on empathy, solidarity, and active engagement with the world's most pressing issues.

Furthermore, this book is a call to action. It encourages readers to move beyond the passive acceptance of the status quo and to embrace their role as agents of change. By reinterpreting Stoic principles in a way that is relevant to today's social and political realities, this book provides a roadmap for those who seek to live with integrity while also working toward a more just and equitable society. In this way, the purpose of the book is twofold: to offer a fresh perspective on an ancient text, and to inspire readers to apply these timeless teachings in ways that address the complexities and challenges of modern life. It's about taking the wisdom of Marcus Aurelius and using it not just as a guide for personal virtue, but as a catalyst for collective transformation.

Ultimately, this book is about more than just philosophy, it's about creating a better world. It's about recognizing that our individual well-being is inextricably linked to the well-being of others, and that by working together, we can create communities that are not only resilient in the face of adversity but also committed to justice, equality, and the preservation of our planet. In the chapters that follow, we will explore how the teachings of Meditations can be reinterpreted to address a range of contemporary issues, from social justice and environmental stewardship to personal growth and community building. The goal is to provide a comprehensive framework for living a life that is both deeply fulfilling and profoundly engaged with the world around us. This book is an invitation to join a journey, a journey that takes us from the ancient halls of Stoic philosophy to the front lines of today's most important struggles. It's a journey that challenges us to rethink what it means to live a good life and to consider how we can use the wisdom of the past to create a more just and equitable future.

Continuing Power Structures

In a world shaped by power structures that often favor a select few, it becomes essential to question and challenge the foundations upon which these structures are built. *Stoic Principles Reimagined for Modern Challenges* is rooted in themes of resistance, resistance against patriarchy, bigotry, and capitalism. These forces have long dictated the terms of our existence, often at the cost of our freedom, our dignity, and our collective well-being. To live authentically in today's world, we must confront these forces head-on, dismantling their hold over our lives and creating space for new ways of being.

Anti-Patriarchy: Reclaiming Our Power

Patriarchy has perpetuated a system where power is equated with control, where strength is measured by dominance, and where value is assigned based on gender. This system has dictated roles, limited opportunities, and justified the subjugation of women and non-binary individuals. In challenging patriarchy, we reclaim our power, not as a means to dominate, but to uplift and support. True power is found in empathy, collaboration, and the recognition that everyone, regardless of gender, has the right to self-determination.

Rejecting patriarchy means embracing equality. It means breaking free from the confines of traditional gender roles and allowing individuals to express their true selves. It means supporting women and non-binary voices, advocating for reproductive rights, and ensuring that all genders have equal opportunities in every sphere of life. It is about creating a society where nurturing, compassion, and cooperation are valued as much as strength, assertiveness, and independence. By dismantling patriarchy, we pave the way for a more inclusive, equitable, and just world.

Anti-Bigotry: Embracing Our Diversity

Bigotry in all its forms, racism, sexism, homophobia, transphobia, ableism, thrives on fear and ignorance. It teaches us to view those who are different as threats rather than as fellow human beings deserving of respect and dignity. To be anti-bigotry is to recognize the beauty and strength in our diversity. It is to see beyond the surface and to value people for who they are, not for the labels society has placed upon them.

Challenging bigotry requires more than passive acceptance; it demands active engagement. It means listening to those who have been marginalized, learning from their experiences, and using our voices to advocate for justice. It means educating ourselves and others, challenging our own biases, and standing up against hate and discrimination in all its forms. By embracing our diversity, we build a society that is rich, vibrant, and reflective of the full spectrum of human experience.

Anti-Capitalism: Prioritizing People and Planet Over Profit

Capitalism has ingrained in us the belief that our value is tied to our productivity, our success to our wealth, and our happiness to our consumption. This system has led to vast inequalities, environmental degradation, and a disconnection from what truly matters. To be anti-capitalist is to challenge to advocate for an economy that serves people, not profits.

An anti-capitalist approach values community, sustainability, and well-being over competition, exploitation, and accumulation. It promotes fair wages, ethical business practices, and the equitable distribution of resources. It recognizes that true prosperity is not about the wealth of a few, but the well-being of all. By prioritizing the needs of people and the planet, we can create an economic system that is just, sustainable, and capable of supporting a thriving society.

Thematic Overview

To fully appreciate the power and relevance of reimagining Meditations in the context of today's world, it's important to first explore the central themes that will guide our journey. These themes form the backbone of this book, each one representing a critical aspect of our lives, both as individuals and as members of a broader community. As we delve into these themes, we'll see how the timeless wisdom of Marcus Aurelius can be adapted to address the most pressing issues of our time.

Personal Responsibility and Social Accountability

One of the core tenets of Stoicism, and indeed one of the most significant aspects of Meditations, is the emphasis on personal responsibility. Marcus Aurelius consistently reflects on the idea that while we cannot control external events, we can control our reactions to them. This focus on self-discipline, on maintaining a calm and rational mind in the face of adversity, is central to Stoic philosophy.

But in reimagining Meditations for the modern world, we need to expand this concept beyond the individual. Personal responsibility remains crucial, but it must be coupled with social accountability. In a world where systemic injustices are rampant, whether in the form of racial discrimination, gender inequality, or economic exploitation, our responsibility extends beyond our own actions and into the realm of how we interact with and challenge these systems. This theme of social accountability invites us to reconsider what it means to live a virtuous life. It's not just about cultivating inner peace; it's about using our personal virtues to engage with the world in a way that promotes justice and equity. It's about recognizing that our actions, or lack thereof, have consequences far beyond ourselves and that true virtue requires us to consider the impact we have on others.

In this book, we'll explore how Marcus's reflections on personal responsibility can be reinterpreted to encourage active participation in social justice efforts. We'll look at how we can use the Stoic principles of rationality, self-discipline, and resilience not just to improve ourselves, but to challenge and transform the societal structures that perpetuate inequality and injustice.

Community and Solidarity Over Individualism

While Stoicism often emphasizes the importance of individual resilience, it's crucial to remember that Marcus Aurelius also acknowledged our interconnectedness as human beings. In Meditations, he frequently reflects on the idea that we are all part of a larger whole, that each person has a role to play in the greater community. This recognition of our shared humanity is a theme that we can build upon in a more progressive interpretation of his work. In today's world, where the ideology of rugged individualism often reigns supreme, it's easy to lose sight of the importance of community and solidarity. We're often told that success is a personal achievement, something we earn through our own hard work and determination. But this narrative overlooks the reality that none of us exist in isolation. Our lives are deeply intertwined with the lives of others, and our well-being is inextricably linked to the well-being of our communities.

This book seeks to shift the focus from individual success to collective well-being. By reinterpreting Marcus's reflections on interconnectedness, we can develop a philosophy that emphasizes the importance of supporting one another, of building communities where everyone has the opportunity to thrive. This is not just about charity or goodwill; it's about recognizing that true strength comes from standing together, from recognizing our shared responsibilities, and from working collaboratively to address the challenges we face.

Through this lens, we'll explore how the concept of solidarity can be woven into the fabric of our daily lives, how we can foster a sense of belonging and mutual support within our communities, and how we can resist the pressures of individualism that seek to divide us. We'll look at examples of how collective action has led to meaningful change, and how we can apply these lessons to build stronger, more resilient communities in the face of today's challenges.

Power, Privilege, and Ethical Leadership

Marcus Aurelius was an emperor, and his writings are infused with reflections on power and leadership. He often grapples with the responsibilities that come with authority, with the challenge of ruling justly and maintaining integrity in the face of immense power. These reflections are particularly relevant today, as we navigate a world where questions of power and privilege are at the forefront of many social and political debates. In reimagining Meditations for a contemporary audience, we must critically examine how power and privilege operate in our lives and in our societies. Marcus's reflections on leadership offer a valuable starting point, but we need to expand the conversation to include a broader understanding of how power dynamics shape our world. This means acknowledging not only the responsibilities of those in positions of authority but also the ways in which privilege, whether based on race, gender, class, or other factors, can influence our perspectives and actions.

This theme invites us to explore the ethical dimensions of power and privilege, asking what it means to lead justly in a world where inequality is often entrenched. It challenges us to consider how we can use whatever power we have, however small, to contribute to positive change. It also calls on us to be aware of the privileges we may hold and to use them responsibly, in service of others rather than for personal gain.

Environmental Stewardship and Living in Accordance with Nature

One of the most profound and perhaps most overlooked aspects of Stoicism is its emphasis on living in accordance with nature. For Marcus Aurelius, this idea was central to his philosophy. He often reflected on the natural order of the universe, the importance of accepting life's cycles, and the need to align one's actions with the rationality and harmony he saw in the world around him. But in the context of the 21st century, where environmental degradation is reaching critical levels, "living in accordance with nature" takes on a new and urgent meaning. Today, our relationship with nature is at a breaking point. The impact of climate change, deforestation, pollution, and the loss of biodiversity is felt worldwide, threatening not just individual species, but the very ecosystems on which all life depends. The Stoic principle of aligning oneself with nature can no longer be just a philosophical exercise; it must become a call to action.

This theme of environmental stewardship reinterprets Marcus's reflections on nature to address our current ecological crisis. It challenges us to rethink our role as stewards of the earth, emphasizing that our moral duty extends beyond human society to include the natural world. This involves recognizing that our well-being is intrinsically linked to the health of the planet and that true virtue requires us to protect and preserve the environment for future generations. By reinterpreting Marcus Aurelius's thoughts on nature through a modern lens, we can develop a philosophy that not only guides our personal lives but also inspires us to act in the fight against climate change and environmental destruction. This is about more than just "going green"; it's about fundamentally rethinking how we live in the world and our responsibilities to the earth and to each other.

Intersectionality and the Interconnectedness of Struggles

Intersectionality is a term that Marcus Aurelius would not have recognized, but the concept is deeply relevant to our reimagining of his work. Coined by scholar Kimberlé Crenshaw in the late 20th century, intersectionality refers to the ways in which different forms of oppression, such as racism, sexism, classism, and others, intersect and compound one another. It's a framework for understanding how various social identities interact to create unique experiences of disadvantage and privilege. Marcus often wrote about the importance of seeing the bigger picture, of understanding how everything in the universe is interconnected. This Stoic perspective can be expanded in our modern context to include a recognition of how different forms of social oppression are intertwined. In today's world, issues like racial injustice, gender inequality, and economic disparity cannot be fully understood or effectively addressed in isolation, they must be approached as part of a broader, interconnected struggle.

This theme of intersectionality invites us to apply Marcus's reflections on interconnectedness to the complex social realities of our time. It challenges us to recognize that the fight for justice is multifaceted and that our efforts to address one form of oppression must consider how it intersects with others. This means not only acknowledging our own social positions and the privileges or disadvantages they confer but also striving to build alliances across different movements for justice. By embracing intersectionality, we can expand Marcus Aurelius's teachings to create a philosophy that is not only personally fulfilling but also deeply attuned to the complexities of social justice in the modern world. It's about moving beyond a singular focus on personal virtue and instead understanding how our lives and struggles are intertwined with those of others.

Finally, we arrive at one of the most crucial themes of this book: the pursuit of justice. For Marcus Aurelius, justice was one of the cardinal virtues, a principle that guided his actions as both an individual and a ruler. He often reflected on the importance of acting justly, of being fair and upright in all his dealings. But in reimagining Meditations for today, we must expand this notion of justice to encompass not just personal integrity, but also the broader societal and systemic dimensions of justice. In our world, the pursuit of justice involves more than just personal fairness; it requires active engagement with the social and political structures that shape our lives. This means recognizing and challenging the injustices that pervade our society, whether they be racial, economic, gender-based, or environmental. It means understanding that justice is not merely an abstract ideal, but a call to action that demands our participation in the work of creating a more equitable world.

This theme will explore how Marcus's reflections on justice can be reinterpreted to inspire meaningful action in the face of modern injustices. We'll discuss the importance of moving beyond contemplation and toward activism, of using our personal virtues as a foundation for engaging with the world in a way that promotes justice and equity. This theme will also examine the role of collective action, the power of movements to create change, and the ways in which individuals can contribute to larger efforts for social and environmental justice. By expanding Marcus Aurelius's concept of justice, this book aims to provide a roadmap for those who seek to live with integrity while also working to create a more just and equitable society. It's about recognizing that the pursuit of justice is not just a personal endeavor, but a collective one, and that our actions, when guided by a commitment to justice, can have a profound impact on the world around us.

Relevance of Marcus Aurelius & Meditations

In the sprawling canon of ancient philosophy, few works have endured with the same influence and relevance as Meditations by Marcus Aurelius. Written nearly two millennia ago, Meditations offers a window into the mind of a Roman emperor who, despite his immense power, was deeply introspective and committed to living a virtuous life. But why, in a world so drastically different from the one Marcus Aurelius knew, should we continue to turn to this ancient text? What makes Meditations more than just a historical artifact, and how can its wisdom speak to us today?

To understand the ongoing relevance of Meditations, it's important to consider both the timeless nature of the themes Marcus Aurelius explores and the unique perspective from which he writes. Marcus was not just a philosopher; he was a ruler tasked with navigating the complexities of leading an empire in turmoil. His reflections were born out of the tension between the demands of his public life and his pursuit of personal integrity. This dual perspective—both deeply personal and profoundly political—imbues Meditations with a unique resonance, particularly for those grappling with the challenges of modern leadership, whether in public service, business, or social movements.

At its core, Meditations is a guide for living a life of virtue in the face of adversity. Marcus Aurelius wrote for himself, reminding himself daily of the principles he believed should govern his actions: wisdom, courage, justice, and temperance. These are the Stoic virtues, and they form the backbone of his philosophy. But beyond these virtues, Marcus also wrestles with the broader questions of existence—how to find peace in a world full of chaos, how to maintain one's integrity in the face of power, and how to reconcile the fleeting nature of life with the pursuit of lasting meaning. These are not just abstract philosophical concerns; they are deeply human ones. They speak to the struggles that all of us, in various forms, continue to face today. In a world that often feels chaotic and overwhelming, the Stoic principles of Meditations offer a way to anchor ourselves, to find steadiness in the midst of life's storms. This is perhaps one of the most enduring aspects of Marcus's work, its ability to provide guidance not just for times of calm, but for moments of crisis.

However, the relevance of Meditations goes beyond its practical advice for personal resilience. In reimagining Marcus Aurelius's work for today, we find that his reflections also offer profound insights into the nature of power, leadership, and ethical responsibility. As a ruler, Marcus was constantly aware of the weight of his decisions, the impact of his actions on the lives of millions. His writings reflect a deep concern for justice, for the well-being of his people, and for the moral obligations that come with power. In this sense, Meditations can be seen as an early exploration of what we might now call ethical leadership. Marcus Aurelius's commitment to ruling justly, to being fair and compassionate even in the face of immense pressure, is a powerful reminder of the responsibilities that come with authority. In today's world, where questions of leadership are more critical than ever, Meditations serves as a timeless guide for those who seek to lead with integrity, whether in government, business, or community organizations.

Moreover, the Stoic emphasis on living in accordance with nature, which runs throughout Meditations, is strikingly relevant in the context of our current environmental challenges. Marcus Aurelius's reflections on the natural order of things, on the interconnectedness of all life, resonate with contemporary concerns about sustainability and ecological responsibility. In an age where the exploitation of the planet's resources has led to a global environmental crisis, the Stoic principle of aligning one's life with the rhythms and limits of nature offers a powerful framework for rethinking our relationship with the earth. Yet, while these elements of Meditations are indeed timeless, their relevance is deepened when we consider the ways in which they can be expanded and adapted to meet the specific challenges of our time. This book seeks to do just that, to take the core principles of Marcus Aurelius's philosophy and reinterpret them through a progressive lens that addresses issues like social justice, environmental stewardship, and the need for collective action in the face of systemic injustice.

For instance, Marcus's reflections on personal responsibility and virtue, while invaluable, must be broadened to include a more explicit recognition of social accountability. By reimagining Meditations in this way, we can create a more holistic approach to Stoicism, one that acknowledges the importance of individual resilience while also emphasizing the need for systemic change. Similarly, the Stoic principle of living in accordance with nature, when viewed through the lens of today's environmental crisis, becomes a call to action for sustainability and ecological justice. Marcus's reflections on the natural world can inspire us to develop a deeper sense of stewardship, recognizing that our well-being is intrinsically linked to the health of the planet. This expanded interpretation of Stoicism can help us navigate the complexities of living responsibly in an age of environmental degradation.

Ultimately, the relevance of Meditations lies not only in its enduring wisdom but in its capacity to be reimagined and adapted to the needs of each generation. In this book, we'll explore how Marcus Aurelius's reflections can be expanded to address the multifaceted challenges of modern life, from the personal to the political, from the ethical to the environmental. By revisiting Meditations with fresh eyes, we can find new ways to apply its teachings in our own lives and in our efforts to create a more just, equitable, and sustainable world. Marcus Aurelius may have lived in a different time, but the questions he grappled with—about how to live well, how to lead justly, and how to find peace in a chaotic world—are as relevant today as they were two thousand years ago.

Modern Reinterpretation

In reimagining Meditations for the 21st century, we're not merely updating an ancient text with a few modern references. We're fundamentally reinterpreting Marcus Aurelius's Stoic philosophy to engage directly with the challenges and complexities of today's world. This reinterpretation is not about dismissing the wisdom of the past but rather expanding it, drawing from the core principles of Stoicism to create a philosophy that resonates with our current social, political, and environmental realities.

Expanding Personal Responsibility to Include Social Accountability

At the core of Stoicism is the idea that we are responsible for our own thoughts, actions, and reactions. Marcus Aurelius's Meditations is filled with reflections on personal responsibility, on the importance of cultivating virtue, maintaining self-discipline, and controlling our responses to the external world. These teachings are timeless and have helped countless individuals navigate life's challenges with grace and integrity. However, in the context of today's interconnected and often unjust world, this focus on personal responsibility can feel incomplete if it is not expanded to include social accountability. The Stoic emphasis on controlling what is within our power must now be interpreted through a broader lens that acknowledges the collective nature of our challenges and the systemic forces that shape our lives.

In a world where inequality, discrimination, and exploitation are pervasive, our personal actions and choices cannot be divorced from their social impact. The modern reinterpretation of Stoicism calls for an understanding that true virtue requires not just personal integrity, but also a commitment to addressing the injustices that affect others. It's about recognizing that we are not isolated individuals, but part of a larger social fabric, and that our responsibility extends beyond ourselves to the communities in which we live. This expanded view of personal responsibility involves a deep engagement with the world around us. It means asking ourselves how our actions contribute to or challenge the status quo, how we can use our resources and privileges to support those who are marginalized, and how we can be allies in the fight for justice. In this reinterpretation, Stoic virtue becomes not just a private pursuit but a public one—an active effort to create a more just and equitable society.

Rethinking the Stoic Concept of "Living in Accordance with Nature"

One of the foundational principles of Stoicism is the idea of living in accordance with nature. For Marcus Aurelius, this meant aligning oneself with the natural order of the universe, accepting the cycles of life and death, and recognizing the rationality and harmony inherent in the world. This principle guided his understanding of fate, mortality, and the importance of maintaining a sense of inner peace amidst life's challenges. In today's context, however, the phrase "living in accordance with nature" takes on a far more urgent and literal meaning. We are living in an era of environmental crisis, where the degradation of the natural world threatens the very survival of life on Earth. Climate change, deforestation, pollution, and the loss of biodiversity are not just abstract concepts, they are realities that impact millions of lives and will shape the future of our planet.

A modern reinterpretation of Stoicism requires us to expand Marcus's idea of living in accordance with nature to include a deep commitment to environmental stewardship. This means recognizing that our actions have consequences not just for ourselves and our communities, but for the planet as a whole. It means understanding that true virtue involves caring for the earth, protecting its resources, and working to restore the balance that has been disrupted by human activity. In this reinterpretation, the Stoic principle of aligning oneself with nature becomes a call to action for sustainability and ecological justice. It challenges us to rethink our relationship with the natural world, to move away from a mindset of exploitation and consumption, and toward one of respect, responsibility, and preservation. By living in accordance with nature in this modern sense, we not only find personal peace but also contribute to the well-being of the planet and future generations.

Reimagining Virtue as a Collective Endeavor

Stoicism traditionally emphasizes the development of personal virtues, wisdom, courage, justice, and temperance, as the path to a good life. Marcus Aurelius devoted much of his Meditations to reflecting on how to cultivate these virtues within himself, often in the face of significant external challenges. He saw virtue as the foundation of a meaningful and fulfilled life, something that could be pursued regardless of one's circumstances. In the context of today's world, the pursuit of virtue remains essential, but it must be reimagined as a collective endeavor rather than just an individual one. The modern reinterpretation of Stoicism acknowledges that while personal virtues are important, they must be practiced in the context of community and collective action. Virtue, in this sense, is not just about personal development but about how we contribute to the common good.

This reimagined concept of virtue recognizes that we are interconnected beings, and that our individual growth is intertwined with the well-being of others. It challenges us to consider how our actions contribute to or detract from the collective flourishing of our communities. It asks us to think about how we can use our strengths and resources to support those around us, how we can stand in solidarity with others in the pursuit of justice, and how we can work together to build a more equitable and compassionate society. In this reinterpretation, virtue becomes a shared responsibility. It's

31

about creating spaces where everyone has the opportunity to thrive, where justice is prioritized, and where the well-being of the community is seen as inseparable from the well-being of the individual. By reimagining virtue in this way, we can build stronger, more resilient communities that are capable of addressing the complex challenges of our time.

Power, Privilege, and Ethical Leadership

Marcus Aurelius was not just a philosopher; he was an emperor, a man who wielded immense power over millions of people. His reflections in Meditations are infused with a deep sense of responsibility and a constant awareness of the ethical implications of his decisions. Marcus's thoughts on leadership were shaped by his position of authority, and his commitment to ruling with justice, humility, and integrity is evident throughout his writings. However, in reinterpreting Meditations for the modern world, we must critically examine how power and privilege operate in our lives today. Marcus Aurelius's reflections on leadership provide a valuable foundation, but in a contemporary context, we need to broaden our understanding of power and privilege to include a recognition of the systemic inequalities that persist in our societies. Ethical leadership in the 21st century requires not only personal integrity but also a commitment to challenging and dismantling the structures of oppression that maintain power imbalances.

This modern reinterpretation of Stoicism emphasizes that leadership is not just about ruling with fairness, it's about actively working to create a more just and equitable world. It calls on those in positions of power to be aware of their privileges and to use them responsibly, in service of the greater good. This means acknowledging the ways in which privilege can blind us to the experiences of others, and making a conscious effort to listen, learn, and act in ways that promote justice and equality. Ethical leadership today also involves recognizing the interconnectedness of our global community. In a world where the decisions of a few can have far-reaching consequences, leaders must consider the impact of their actions on both the local and global scales. This requires a commitment to principles of fairness, transparency, and accountability, as well as a willingness to prioritize the well-being of people and the planet over personal or corporate gain.

Emotional Resilience and the Importance of Community Care

One of the hallmarks of Stoic philosophy is its emphasis on emotional resilience, the idea that we should cultivate the ability to remain calm, composed, and rational in the face of adversity. Marcus Aurelius often reminded himself to accept what he could not change, to detach from the emotional turmoil of external events, and to focus on maintaining inner peace. This focus on emotional resilience has made Stoicism particularly appealing to those seeking ways to cope with the stresses and uncertainties of life. However, in the modern reinterpretation of Stoicism, we must recognize that emotional resilience is not just an individual endeavor, it is deeply connected to the support and care we receive from our communities. The idea of "going it alone" in the pursuit of emotional strength can be isolating and counterproductive, especially in a world where mental health challenges are increasingly prevalent and where many people feel disconnected and unsupported.

This reinterpretation emphasizes the importance of community care as a foundation for emotional resilience. It acknowledges that while Stoicism encourages us to cultivate inner strength, true resilience often requires the support of others. We are social beings, and our ability to cope with life's challenges is strengthened when we have a network of caring, empathetic individuals who can offer support, guidance, and companionship. Community care involves creating environments where people feel safe, valued, and supported, where they can share their struggles without fear of judgment and where they can find the resources they need to heal and grow. It's about recognizing that our individual well-being is tied to the well-being of those around us, and that by fostering a culture of care, we can build more resilient communities.

The Role of Reflection and Self-Awareness in Personal and Social Transformation

Reflection and self-awareness are central to Stoic practice. Marcus Aurelius frequently used Meditations as a tool for introspection, recording his thoughts, examining his actions, and reminding himself of the principles he aimed to live by. This practice of regular self-reflection allowed him to stay grounded in his values, to identify areas where he needed to grow, and to maintain a sense of purpose and direction in his life. In today's fast-paced world, where distractions are constant and the pressure to keep moving forward can be overwhelming, the practice of reflection is more important than ever. Self-awareness and reflection can contribute not just to personal transformation, but also to social change.

This reinterpretation emphasizes that reflection is not merely an individual exercise, it's a critical component of our collective efforts to create a more just and equitable society. By engaging in regular self-reflection, we can become more aware of our own biases, privileges, and blind spots. We can identify the ways in which our actions and behaviors contribute to or challenge the status quo, and we can make more conscious choices that align with our values and with the broader goals of social justice. Moreover, reflection can help us develop greater empathy and understanding for others. By taking the time to consider different perspectives, to listen deeply to those whose experiences differ from our own, and to reflect on the impact of our words and actions, we can cultivate a more inclusive and compassionate approach to both personal interactions.

Connection to Current Social Issues

As we delve deeper into the modern reinterpretation of Meditations, it's essential to ground these philosophical reflections in the concrete realities of our time. The strength of Marcus Aurelius's writings lies in their universality, their ability to speak to the human condition across the ages. However, the true power of reimagining Meditations today comes from directly linking its principles to the pressing social issues that define our world. By making these connections, we can transform ancient wisdom into a living philosophy, one that not only guides individual actions but also drives collective change.

Social Justice and Equality

In today's world, social justice is at the forefront of many movements and conversations. Issues such as racial discrimination, gender inequality, LGBTQ+ rights, and economic disparity are not just abstract concerns, they are lived realities for millions of people. These issues challenge us to consider how the principles of justice and fairness, as discussed by Marcus Aurelius, can be applied in ways that actively address these systemic inequities. Marcus Aurelius's reflections on justice emphasize the importance of treating others with fairness and acting with integrity. However, in a modern context, justice must be understood as more than just personal fairness, it must involve a commitment to dismantling the systems of oppression that create and perpetuate inequality. This means recognizing the privileges that some of us hold and using them to advocate for those who are marginalized. It means not just thinking about justice in our personal dealings, but also working to ensure that our institutions and societies are just and equitable for all.

The connection between Meditations and social justice becomes particularly relevant when we consider the Stoic emphasis on the common good. Marcus Aurelius often wrote about the interconnectedness of all people and the idea that we are all part of a larger community. In today's world, this concept calls us to acknowledge our shared humanity and to take responsibility for creating a society that is inclusive and fair. By applying Stoic principles to modern social justice movements, we can develop a philosophy that not only helps us navigate our own lives but also contributes to the broader struggle for equality and human rights.

Environmental Crisis and Sustainability

One of the most pressing issues of our time is the environmental crisis. Climate change, deforestation, pollution, and the loss of biodiversity are not just environmental problems, they are existential threats that affect every aspect of life on Earth. The connection between Meditations and environmental sustainability may not seem obvious at first, but upon closer examination, the Stoic principle of living in accordance with nature provides a powerful framework for addressing these challenges. Marcus Aurelius often reflected on the natural world and the importance of aligning one's life with the rhythms and cycles of nature. For the Stoics, living in harmony with nature was not just about accepting the world as it is, but about understanding our place within it and acting in ways that respect the natural order. In today's context, this principle can be reinterpreted as a call to environmental stewardship, a recognition that our well-being is intrinsically linked to the health of the planet.

The modern environmental movement emphasizes the need for sustainable practices, the protection of natural resources, and the urgent need to reduce our impact on the Earth. By connecting these goals with the Stoic idea of living in accordance with nature, we can create a philosophy that not only promotes personal resilience but also encourages active participation in the fight against environmental degradation. This connection between ancient wisdom and modern environmentalism can inspire individuals to adopt more sustainable lifestyles, support policies that protect the environment, and engage in collective actions that aim to preserve the planet for future generations.

Mental Health and Community Care

Mental health is another critical issue that has gained increasing attention in recent years. The pressures of modern life, coupled with the isolation, stress, and uncertainty brought about by global events, have led to a widespread mental health crisis. In this context, the Stoic focus on emotional resilience and inner peace is particularly relevant, but it must be adapted to address the complexities of mental health in the contemporary world. Marcus Aurelius wrote extensively about the importance of maintaining a calm and rational mind, of accepting what we cannot change, and of finding peace within ourselves. These ideas are foundational to Stoic practice, but in today's world, where mental health issues are prevalent, it's crucial to expand this focus to include community care. Emotional resilience is not something we can or should cultivate in isolation, it is strengthened by the support we receive from others and by the communities we build around us.

The connection between Meditations and modern mental health practices lies in the integration of Stoic principles with contemporary understandings of community care and mutual support. While Stoicism encourages self-reflection and personal growth, it also reminds us of the importance of our relationships with others. In a world where many people struggle with feelings of loneliness, anxiety, and depression, fostering strong, supportive communities is essential. By linking Stoic resilience with the concept of community care, we can create a holistic approach to mental health that emphasizes both individual well-being and the collective support systems that sustain it.

This modern reinterpretation of Stoicism, grounded in the

realities of today's social issues, offers a way to make ancient wisdom relevant and actionable in the 21st century. By connecting Meditations to the challenges of social justice, environmental sustainability, and mental health, we can develop a philosophy that is not only personally enriching but also socially transformative. Through these connections, we can see how the principles that guided Marcus Aurelius in his time can still guide us today helping us to navigate the complexities of modern life with wisdom, compassion, and a commitment to making the world a better place for all.

A Push for Change

As we reach the end of this introduction, it's time to reflect on the purpose of revisiting and reinterpreting Meditations by Marcus Aurelius. This is not simply an intellectual exercise or a journey into the past for its own sake. It is, fundamentally, a call to action—a challenge to take the timeless wisdom of Stoicism and use it as a force for good in the world today. The teachings of Marcus Aurelius offer us more than just a guide to personal virtue; they provide a blueprint for how to engage with the world around us in meaningful ways. But the philosophy he espoused, while powerful, is not static. It must evolve, adapt, and expand to meet the needs of each new generation. The reinterpretation we have begun here is about making Stoicism relevant, actionable, and transformative in the context of the 21st century.

This call to action is twofold: it challenges us to apply these reimagined Stoic principles to our own lives and to use them as a foundation for creating positive change in the world. The first step is introspective. It asks you to reflect deeply on the values that guide your actions, to cultivate a sense of personal responsibility that extends beyond your individual concerns, and to develop the emotional resilience needed to face life's challenges with courage and clarity. But introspection alone is not enough. The second, and equally critical, step is outward facing. It's about translating your personal growth into collective action. It's about recognizing that the pursuit of virtue must be intertwined with the pursuit of justice, that true wisdom is found not only in contemplation but in active engagement with the world's most pressing issues.

So, what does this look like in practice?

It looks like committing to social justice in all its forms, standing up against racism, sexism, and all forms of discrimination, and using your voice and resources to support those who are marginalized. It looks like taking a stand for environmental sustainability, making conscious choices in your daily life to reduce your impact on the planet, and advocating for policies that protect the Earth for future generations. It looks like building and participating in communities of care, offering support to those who struggle with mental health, fostering connections that combat loneliness, and creating spaces where everyone feels valued and heard. It's about recognizing that we are stronger together and that our resilience is magnified when we stand in solidarity with others.

This call to action is about moving beyond passive acceptance of the status quo and embracing your role as an agent of change. It's about taking the principles of Stoicism, principles of justice, wisdom, courage, and temperance, and applying them in ways that challenge the injustices and inequalities that persist in our world. It's about being brave enough to question the structures of power and privilege, and being committed enough to work towards creating a society that is truly just and equitable.

Moreover, it's about doing all of this with the humility and self-awareness that Marcus Aurelius himself so often espoused. It's about recognizing that while we may strive for virtue, we will not always achieve it perfectly, and that's okay. The goal is not perfection, but progress. The call to action is not about achieving an ideal state of being but about committing to the ongoing work of bettering ourselves and the world around us. As you move forward, take these teachings to heart. Let them guide you, inspire you, and challenge you. Let them push you out of your comfort zone and into spaces where real change can happen. And remember, this journey is not one you undertake alone.

We are all part of a larger community, a global collective that is interconnected in ways Marcus Aurelius could only have imagined. Together, we can make a difference. Together, we can live according to the principles of Stoic wisdom while also transforming our world for the better. The time to act is now. The world needs individuals who are not only wise and virtuous in their private lives but who are also courageous and committed in the public sphere. This is your call to action: to take the lessons of Meditations and reimagine them in ways that resonate with the challenges and opportunities of today. By doing so, you can help build a future that is more just, more compassionate, and more sustainable for all.

In Closing

As we conclude this introduction, it's worth taking a moment to reflect on the journey we're about to undertake together. *Stoic Principles Reimagined for Modern Challenges* looks at reimagining Meditations by Marcus Aurelius for the modern world as not just an intellectual exercise, but as an invitation to engage with ancient wisdom in a way that is both deeply personal and profoundly relevant to the challenges of our time. Throughout this book, we've set out to explore how the Stoic principles articulated by Marcus Aurelius, principles of virtue, wisdom, and resilience, can be adapted to address the complexities of contemporary life. But more than that, we've aimed to show that these principles, when reinterpreted through a progressive lens, have the power to inspire real and meaningful change, both within ourselves and in the world around us.

The Stoic emphasis on personal responsibility, on living a life of virtue despite the chaos of the external world, remains as crucial today as it was two thousand years ago. But as we've discussed, in the context of our modern world, this personal responsibility must extend beyond the self. It must include a commitment to social justice, environmental stewardship, and the well-being of our communities. This reinterpretation of Stoicism challenges us to think beyond our individual lives and to consider how our actions contribute to the collective good. In many ways, the principles that Marcus Aurelius reflected upon in his writings were timeless, they spoke to the human condition in ways that resonate across the centuries. But the world we live in today presents new challenges and new complexities that Marcus could not have anticipated. Climate change, systemic inequality, global interconnectedness, these are issues that require us to expand the Stoic framework, to think critically about how we can apply ancient wisdom to the unique circumstances of our time.

As you move through the chapters of this book, I encourage you to approach these teachings with both an open mind and a critical eye. Allow yourself to be challenged by the ideas presented here, but also take the time to reflect on how they resonate with your own experiences. Stoicism is not a one-size-fits-all philosophy, it's a toolkit that each of us can use in our own way, adapting its principles to fit the contours of our lives and the needs of our communities. Remember, too, that this journey is not one of perfection. Marcus Aurelius himself often wrote about his own shortcomings, his struggles to live up to the ideals he held so dear. He understood that the pursuit of virtue is a lifelong endeavor, one marked by setbacks and failures as well as successes. The same is true for us today. The process of integrating these Stoic principles into our lives, of reimagining them for the modern world, will be imperfect. But it is in this imperfection that growth happens, that learning takes place, and that real transformation can occur.

The world today is in desperate need of individuals who are not only committed to personal growth but also to the betterment of society. We need leaders who are guided by ethical principles, communities that are built on mutual support and care, and a collective movement toward justice and sustainability. This book is not just a guide for living a good life, it's a call to be part of something larger, to use the wisdom of the past as a foundation for building a better future.

As we close this introduction and begin the journey through the pages that follow, I want to leave you with a simple yet powerful reminder: You have the capacity to make a difference. Whether it's in your personal life, in your community, or on a larger scale, the principles you cultivate within yourself can ripple outward, affecting the world in ways you may never fully see or understand. By embracing the teachings of Meditations, reinterpreted for the challenges of today, you can become a force for good in a world that desperately needs it.

So, as you turn the page and dive deeper into the wisdom of

Marcus Aurelius, remember that this is not just a journey of the mind, but a journey of the heart and soul. It's about finding your place in the world, understanding the impact you can have, and committing to a life of purpose, integrity, and action. Together, we can take the timeless wisdom of Stoicism and use it to create a more just, equitable, and sustainable world, one thought, one action, one person at a time.

Esme Mees, Summer 2024

Unremarkable 2, 2024

Book 1

Cultivating Wisdom from Others

1. From my mother, I learned the strength of gentle words,
Words that heal, words that bind wounds unseen,
In a world often ruled by force and might,
She showed me that true power lies in understanding,
In the embrace that shelters, in the voice that soothes,
A love untainted by the cruel chains of power,
Where every individual is seen not as a tool,
But as a being of intrinsic worth,
Worthy of dignity, respect, and care.

2. My father, a man of simple means,
Taught me the value of humility and honor,
Not in the accumulation of wealth or title,
But in the authenticity of one's actions,
To walk through life with integrity as my guide,
Seeing each person not by their status or name,
But by the content of their character,
To cherish each life and every divergent view,
And to hold empathy as the highest virtue.

3. A mentor, wise beyond their years,
Showed me the strength to stand against the tides,
To question the patriarchal structures built,
Not to conform but to reshape, to reform,
For justice is not something granted from above,
It is forged in the fires of resistance,
Owned not by a few, but a collective right,
To dismantle the chains, to shatter the glass,
And build a world anew, where all voices are heard.

4. From friends who faced bigotry's harsh hand,
I learned resilience, the power of solidarity,

To see beyond the color of skin, the beliefs held,
To the humanity that binds us all,
Their stories of struggle, of pain and triumph,
Taught me to rise, to speak, to never be silent,
For silence is complicity, a weapon of the oppressor,
In our unity lies strength, in our diversity, power,
To break the cycle of hate, to pave the way for love.

5. The elders, with years etched into their faces,
Taught me to value the wisdom of shared experiences,
To look beyond the superficial promises of capitalism,
To the community that thrives on compassion,
Where success is not measured by wealth amassed,
But by the lives touched, the kindness shown,
To build a world where resources are shared,
Where everyone's needs are met, and no one goes hungry,
For in this lies true prosperity, true wealth.

6. From the laughter of children, pure and unfiltered,
I learned the essence of freedom, unchained,
A world unburdened by the past's prejudices,
Where dreams soar high, untainted by fear,
Their innocence a beacon, guiding us forward,
To a society built not on division,
But on the celebration of each unique spirit,
Where joy is found in the simple, the everyday,
Not in conquest, but in the beauty of being alive.

7. The poets, with their verses, painted worlds unseen,
Dreams of a future where humanity transcends greed,
Where every person, every creature, finds its place,
In a tapestry woven from love, from shared purpose,
To envision a reality where exploitation is no more,
Where the earth is not a resource to be drained,
But a home to be cherished, to be protected,
For every poem is a revolution, a call to arms,
Against the tide of materialism, towards a life of meaning.

8. From healers, I learned the sanctity of life,
The importance of nurturing, of mending,
That strength is not in the sword, but in the hand that heals,
In the heart that opens, in the care that is given freely,
They showed me that every life is precious,
A flame that deserves to burn bright,
Not snuffed out by neglect, by indifference,
But fed by compassion, by the will to see others thrive,
For in healing others, we heal ourselves.

9. The artists, with colors bold, with lines that speak,
Taught me to see the world in its myriad hues,
To celebrate the differences that make us whole,
For beauty lies not in uniformity, but in diversity,
They paint a vision of a world where all are free,
Not bound by the chains of societal norms,
Where creativity flourishes, unburdened by the market's
demands,
A testament to the power of the human spirit,
To create, to inspire, to bring forth change.

10. The rebels, those who dared to dream differently,
Showed me the power of defiance, of saying no,
To a world that demands conformity, obedience,
They stood tall, voices raised, hands joined,
Against the tide of oppression, the darkness of tyranny,
For every act of rebellion is a spark,
A light in the darkness, a promise of hope,
That change is possible, that a better world awaits,
If we dare to fight, to dream, to believe.

11. From philosophers who pondered the depths of life,
I learned that wisdom is not found in certainty,
But in the questions that provoke thought,
In the courage to doubt, to challenge the norm,
For knowledge is not a weapon to dominate,
But a torch to light the way to truth,
It is in the relentless pursuit of understanding,

That we dismantle ignorance and build bridges,
Where minds can meet, debate, and evolve together.

12. The activists who walked the streets, voices raised,
Taught me that justice is not a gift bestowed,
But a right demanded, a struggle ongoing,
In every protest, every march, lies the heartbeat,
Of a world crying out for change, for fairness,
For they know that rights are not written in stone,
But fought for, earned, and fiercely protected,
Their courage a beacon, their sacrifice a call,
To stand up, to speak out, to fight for what is just.

13. From the earth beneath my feet, solid and ancient,
I learned the value of simplicity, of roots,
To honor the land, not as a resource to exploit,
But as a mother that nurtures, that gives life,
In the cycles of nature, I see a truth profound,
That life is interconnected, each being part of the whole,
To live in harmony with the land, not in dominion,
For in the balance of give and take lies peace,
A lesson that all must learn, before it is too late.

14. The martyrs, whose voices were silenced,
Yet whose spirits live on, stronger than before,
Taught me that some causes are worth any price,
That freedom, justice, and truth are worth dying for,
Their blood, a seed, from which grows the resolve,
To fight on, to carry forward their mission,
For every life lost in the name of justice,
Becomes a rallying cry, a beacon of hope,
Reminding us that the fight is never in vain.

15. From the dreamers who look to the stars,
I learned to envision a world unbounded,
Beyond the limitations imposed by fear,
Where possibilities are endless, and hope is real,
They teach us that imagination is a powerful tool,

A means to break free from the chains of the present,
To see beyond what is, to what could be,
A world where justice flows like a river,
And freedom is not a privilege, but a birthright.

16. The silent ones, whose pain is hidden,
Taught me to listen with my heart, not just my ears,
To hear the stories that go untold,
To see the struggles that are overlooked,
For every silence speaks volumes,
Every quiet moment a plea for understanding,
In the stillness, there is a power, a truth,
That we must recognize and honor,
For it is often the quietest voices that hold the deepest truths.

17. From scholars who delved into ancient texts,
I learned the importance of history, of memory,
To know where we have come from,
To understand the patterns, the cycles,
For in the past lie lessons, warnings,
Of what happens when greed overtakes compassion,
When power is concentrated in the hands of a few,
To learn from the mistakes, to build a future better,
A world informed by wisdom, by the lessons of time.

18. From the whispers of the future, I heard a call,
To act, to make a difference here and now,
For the future is not a distant dream,
But a reality shaped by our choices today,
To take the path less traveled, to stand for what is right,
To break free from the chains of conformity,
And to forge a world where equity is the norm,
Where every life is valued, every voice heard,
A world we can be proud to pass on.

Unremarkable 3, 2024

Book 2

Embracing the Present, Challenging the Norms

1. Embrace this moment, for it is all we truly have,
The past is a shadow, the future a dream,
Here, now, in this breath, is where life unfolds,
In the beating of hearts, in the rhythm of time,
To live fully is to be present,
To see the world not through the lens of what was,
Or what could be, but what is,
To ground oneself in reality,
And find peace in the truth of now.

2. Challenge the norms that bind and blind,
For they are but constructs of a time gone by,
Rules written to serve the few,
To keep the masses in line, unquestioning,
But we are not born to follow blindly,
We are beings of thought, of reason,
To question is to live, to doubt is to grow,
For it is in the challenge that we find ourselves,
In the breaking of chains, we discover freedom.

3. The present is a gift, not a burden,
A chance to make a difference, to be,
In the face of adversity, in the light of joy,
To seize the day, to shape our destiny,
Not bound by the fears of tomorrow,
Nor the regrets of yesterday,
But grounded in the here, the now,
For life is fleeting, a moment, a breath,
And in each breath, lies the power to change.

4. The norms of society, the rules unspoken,
Are not the laws of nature, but of man,

Constructed to maintain the status quo,
To benefit those who hold the reins,
But we are more than cogs in a machine,
We are creators, innovators, rebels,
To challenge the norm is to seek truth,
To defy the unjust, to speak for the silenced,
And in defiance, we find our strength.

5. To live in the present is to live authentically,
To embrace each moment with open eyes,
Not clouded by the illusions of control,
Or the false promises of permanence,
Life is ever-changing, a river in flow,
To resist is to suffer, to embrace is to be free,
For in acceptance lies the key to peace,
And in peace, the foundation of a life well-lived,
A life not bound by the past, nor fearful of the future.

6. Question the roles you are told to play,
The masks you are asked to wear,
For they are not the essence of who you are,
But the expectations of a world not yours,
To conform is to lose oneself,
To fit in is to fade away,
But to stand apart, to be true,
Is to embrace the uniqueness within,
And in that uniqueness, find power.

7. The present is a canvas, blank and pure,
A space to create, to dream, to act,
Not confined by the rules of those before,
But open to the possibilities of now,
To paint a life of meaning, of purpose,
To leave a mark, not of conformity,
But of individuality, of truth,
For it is in the act of creation,
That we find our place, our voice.

8. The norms of the past are the chains of today,
Forged in the fires of fear, of control,
But we are not prisoners, bound by fate,
We are the authors of our own story,
To write a new chapter, a new narrative,
Where equality is the rule, not the exception,
Where justice is not a dream, but a reality,
To break the chains, to forge new paths,
And in those paths, find liberation.

9. To live in the present is to embrace uncertainty,
To see the world not in black and white,
But in shades of grey, of color, of light,
For life is not a straight line, but a journey,
A path winding, unpredictable,
To fear the unknown is to miss the adventure,
To embrace it is to live fully,
For in each twist, each turn, lies discovery,
And in discovery, the essence of life.

10. Challenge the structures that divide and oppress,
For they are not natural, but constructed,
To maintain power, to subjugate, to control,
But we are not born to be divided,
We are born to be united,
To see beyond the barriers, the walls,
To the humanity that connects us all,
For in unity, there is strength,
And in strength, the power to change the world.

11. The present is not just a moment, but a choice,
To act, to speak, to be,
To stand for what is right, even in the face of fear,
To be a voice for the voiceless, a light in the dark,
For each action, each word, echoes through time,
Creating ripples, waves, of change,
To live is to choose, and to choose is to live,

Not in the shadows of others,
But in the light of one's own truth

12. Challenge the myths that bind our minds,
The lies of scarcity, of competition,
For there is enough for all, if we but share,
To see each other not as rivals, but as kin,
In the abundance of nature, in the richness of life,
There is a place for everyone,
To live in harmony, not in conflict,
To build a world not of greed, but of love,
And in that love, find our true humanity.

13. The present moment calls for courage,
To face the reality before us without illusion,
To accept both joy and sorrow as part of life,
For it is in the full embrace of all experiences,
That we find resilience, the strength to endure,
To see each challenge not as an obstacle,
But as a chance to grow, to learn, to transform,
For every moment, whether light or dark,
Is a teacher, guiding us to wisdom.

14. Reject the comfort of complacency,
For it is a trap that dulls the mind,
A false sense of safety that keeps us bound,
To routines, to traditions that no longer serve,
To be alive is to be aware,
To question, to seek, to strive,
For complacency breeds stagnation,
But the spirit thrives in the pursuit of truth,
In the challenge of becoming more than we are.

15. The present is not a place to hide,
But a space to engage, to participate,
To be part of the world, not apart from it,
For in isolation, there is no growth,
But in connection, in community,

There lies the power to make a difference,
To touch lives, to change hearts,
For each interaction is an opportunity,
To bring light, to bring love.

16. Challenge the idols of power and wealth,
For they are but shadows, illusions,
True power lies not in control,
But in the ability to uplift, to empower,
Wealth is not in possessions amassed,
But in the richness of relationships,
To value people over profit,
To see success not in numbers,
But in the lives we impact, the love we give.

17. Embrace the uncertainty of the present,
For it is the canvas upon which life is painted,
Each moment a brushstroke, each decision a color,
To fear the unknown is to miss the beauty,
To control is to limit, to release is to expand,
For life is a dance, a flow, ever-changing,
And in that flow, we find our rhythm,
A harmony that comes not from control,
But from acceptance, from trust.

18. Question the purpose of tradition,
Not all that is old is wise,
Not all that is ancient is true,
For the world evolves, as do we,
To cling to the past is to deny the future,
To embrace change is to welcome growth,
For in the evolution of thought,
In the progression of society,
We find the potential for a better world.

19. The present is a stage, and we are the actors,
Each with a role to play, a story to tell,
But the script is not written, the ending not set,

We have the power to improvise, to create,
To write a narrative not of conformity,
But of freedom, of possibility,
To act with integrity, to speak with truth,
For in our actions, we shape the world,
In our words, we build the future.

20. Challenge the fear of failure,
For failure is not the end, but a beginning,
A step on the path, a lesson learned,
For it is not the fall that defines us,
But the rise, the return, the resilience,
To fail is to be human, to grow is divine,
To embrace each setback as a teacher,
To see each mistake as an opportunity,
For in the process, we find our strength.

21. The present is a gift, not of time, but of choice,
To choose to live, to choose to be,
To choose to see the world as it is,
And to dream of what it could be,
For every moment holds the potential,
To change a life, to shift a paradigm,
To be a force of good, a beacon of hope,
To live not just for oneself,
But for the betterment of all.

22. Challenge the belief that we are alone,
For in every being, there is a spark,
A connection, a thread that binds,
To see each other not as strangers,
But as kin, as companions on this journey,
For we are all part of the same whole,
Each life a note in the symphony,
To live in harmony, to walk in peace,
To build a world of unity, of love.

23. The present moment is an invitation to be authentic,
To shed the masks we wear for acceptance,
To step out of the roles assigned by others,
And into the truth of who we are,
For authenticity is the foundation of a fulfilled life,
To be true to oneself is to honor the self,
To stand firm in one's beliefs,
Even when the world demands conformity,
For the power of being real is the power to inspire.

24. Challenge the narratives that divide us,
The stories that pit us against one another,
For they are the tools of those who fear unity,
To keep us isolated, fearful, alone,
But we are not enemies, we are allies,
Each one of us a thread in the tapestry of life,
To tear down the walls of prejudice, of hate,
To build bridges of understanding, of respect,
For in unity, there is strength, in diversity, beauty.

25. The present moment is a canvas for change,
Not a space to merely exist,
But a stage to act, to create, to transform,
For each moment holds the potential,
To reshape the narrative, to rewrite the script,
To challenge what is, with what could be,
To see the world not as a fixed entity,
But as a living, breathing possibility,
For in each moment, there is the power to redefine.

Unremarkable 4, 2024

Book 3

Integrity and Shared Consciousness

1. Integrity is the anchor of the soul,
To act with honesty, even when unseen,
To be true to one's word, steadfast in commitment,
For a life of integrity is a life of peace,
Where the mind is not burdened by deceit,
And the heart is not heavy with guilt,
To live with integrity is to walk a path,
Clear of doubt, open to the light,
For it is in truth that we find our strength.

2. In the quiet of the mind, there lies wisdom,
To know oneself, to understand one's desires,
Is to navigate life with clarity,
Not swayed by the whims of others,
But guided by the compass of conscience,
For the greatest power is self-mastery,
To control one's thoughts, one's actions,
To act not out of impulse, but out of principle,
For integrity is the light that guides.

3. The shared consciousness is our common humanity,
A web of connection, of empathy,
To see oneself in the other,
To feel the pain, the joy, the hope,
For we are not isolated beings,
But part of a larger whole,
To live for oneself is a lonely path,
But to live for others is to find meaning,
For in giving, we receive; in others, we find ourselves.

4. To embrace integrity is to reject hypocrisy,
To live by the values we profess,

For words without action are empty,
A facade that crumbles with time,
To act with consistency, with authenticity,
Is to earn trust, to build respect,
For it is in the alignment of word and deed,
That we find the essence of character,
The foundation of a life well-lived.

5. The strength of a community lies in its unity,
In the bonds forged through shared purpose,
For no one is an island, complete in themselves,
We are all threads in the tapestry of existence,
To pull one thread is to affect the whole,
To care for others is to care for oneself,
For in the collective, we find strength,
In the collective, we find purpose,
To work together, to build together, to thrive.

6. Integrity demands courage, the strength to stand,
Against the tide of corruption, of deceit,
To be a voice of reason in a world of noise,
To speak truth to power, to challenge the false,
For it is not the loudest voice that prevails,
But the one that speaks with conviction,
To hold fast to the truth, even when it is hard,
For in courage, we find the path to justice,
In courage, we find the path to change.

7. The shared consciousness is a force for good,
When guided by compassion, by empathy,
To see beyond the self, to the needs of others,
To act not out of self-interest,
But out of a sense of shared responsibility,
For we are all part of the same human family,
To lift one is to lift all,
To harm one is to harm all,
For in the collective, we find our humanity.

8. Integrity is not a virtue of convenience,
But a commitment to be upheld,
In times of ease and in times of trial,
To be steadfast in the face of temptation,
For a life of integrity is a life of honor,
A life that leaves a legacy,
Not of wealth or power,
But of respect, of trust,
For it is the integrity of one that inspires many.

9. In the shared consciousness, there is power,
The power to create, to build, to transform,
For when people come together with a shared vision,
There is no limit to what can be achieved,
To harness the power of the collective,
Is to recognize the potential of each individual,
To value each voice, each contribution,
For in diversity, there is strength,
In unity, there is power.

10. To live with integrity is to live without fear,
For fear is the companion of deceit,
The shadow that lurks in the dark,
But in the light of truth, fear dissipates,
For there is nothing to hide, nothing to conceal,
To be honest, is to be free,
Free from the chains of lies,
Free from the burden of guilt,
For in integrity, there is liberation.

11. The shared consciousness is a mirror,
Reflecting the values of society,
To see injustice is to recognize the need for change,
To see suffering is to feel the call to act,
For we are not passive observers of life,
But active participants,
To change the world is to change ourselves,
To change ourselves is to change the world,

For in the collective, we find the power to shape our destiny.

12. Integrity is the foundation of trust,
The bedrock upon which relationships are built,
To be trustworthy is to be reliable,
To be reliable is to be respected,
For trust is not given, but earned,
Through actions, through consistency,
To live with integrity is to live a life of meaning,
A life that impacts, that inspires,
For it is in integrity that we find our true self.

13. To act with integrity is to honor the self,
Not to be swayed by the opinions of others,
For the approval of many is fleeting,
But the approval of one's conscience is eternal,
To stand firm in one's convictions,
Even when the world turns away,
For it is better to be alone in truth,
Than to be surrounded by falsehood,
For in truth, there is strength; in lies, weakness.

14. The shared consciousness is not a burden,
But a gift, a reminder that we are not alone,
In a world that often feels isolating,
To know that we are part of something larger,
To share in the joys, the sorrows of others,
For empathy is the thread that binds,
To feel for another is to connect,
To connect is to heal,
For in the collective, we find comfort, solace.

15. Integrity is not about perfection,
But about authenticity,
To be flawed is to be human,
To admit mistakes is to be wise,
For it is not the absence of error,
But the willingness to learn, to grow,

To be honest with oneself,
To accept both strengths and weaknesses,
For in acceptance, there is humility, in humility, growth.

16. The power of the shared is in its diversity,
In the multitude of perspectives, of experiences,
For it is in the differences that we find innovation,
To listen is to learn, to understand,
For no single mind holds all truth,
No single voice speaks for all,
To value each contribution is to build strength,
To embrace each difference is to build unity,
For in diversity, there is richness; in unity, power.

17. To live with integrity is to live with purpose,
To have a guiding principle, a north star,
For a life without purpose is adrift,
A ship without a rudder,
To know one's values, one's goals,
Is to navigate life with direction,
To act not out of compulsion, but choice,
For in purpose, there is clarity; in clarity, peace.

18. The shared consciousness is a vision of a better world,
A world where all are seen, all are valued,
Where no one is left behind,
Where the success of one is the success of all,
To work towards this vision is to live with hope,
To live with hope is to inspire,
For a world united is a world strong,
A world of compassion, of care,
For in the collective, we find our future; in unity, our strength.

Unremarkable 5, 2024

Book 4

Confronting Power, Achieving Change

1. Power is not inherently virtuous;
It is defined by how it is wielded,
To hold power is to bear responsibility,
For the well-being of others, for justice,
Yet too often it is used for control,
To maintain hierarchies, to silence dissent,
True power lies not in domination,
But in the courage to uplift, to empower,
For in empowering others, we find our own strength.

2. The status quo thrives on silence,
On the acceptance of what is,
But change begins with questioning,
With the refusal to accept injustice,
To challenge power is to disrupt the comfort,
To stir the waters, to awaken minds,
For in the stillness of conformity,
There is stagnation, there is decay,
But in the challenge, there is life, there is growth.

3. Power seeks to divide, to isolate,
For in division lies control,
To pit one against the other,
To foster fear, distrust, suspicion,
But the strength of the people is in unity,
In the collective voice, the shared dream,
To unite is to challenge the powerful,
To break the chains of oppression,
For in unity, there is hope, there is change.

4. True change is not in grand gestures,
But in the small, consistent actions,

In the daily choices that reflect values,
In the words spoken, the deeds done,
To live with integrity in a world of compromise,
To hold to principles in a world of corruption,
For it is the accumulation of these acts,
That builds the foundation of a new world,
A world where justice reigns, where truth is honored.

5. The power of change lies in the vision,
The ability to see beyond the present,
To imagine a world not as it is,
But as it could be,
To dream of a society built on equity,
On compassion, on shared prosperity,
For it is not enough to resist,
We must also create,
For in creation, there is transformation, there is possibility.

6. Confront the power that exploits,
That takes without giving, that hoards without sharing,
For exploitation is a cycle, a system,
A chain that binds both the oppressed and the oppressor,
To break free is to redefine success,
Not in terms of wealth or power,
But in terms of impact, of legacy,
To create a world where all can thrive,
Where wealth is shared, and power is just.

7. The first step in creating change is awareness,
To see the world as it is,
To recognize the injustices, the inequalities,
To understand the systems that perpetuate them,
For in awareness, there is awakening,
A call to action, a call to conscience,
To no longer be complicit, to no longer be blind,
For in seeing, there is responsibility,
And in responsibility, there is the power to change.

8. To confront power is to confront fear,
For fear is the tool of the powerful,
To keep the people in line, to keep them quiet,
But courage is not the absence of fear,
It is the choice to act in spite of it,
To speak when silence is expected,
To stand when sitting is safer,
For it is in the courageous act,
That we find the seeds of revolution, of change.

9. The power of change lies in solidarity,
In the coming together of voices, of hearts,
For one voice can be silenced,
But a chorus cannot,
To stand together is to stand strong,
To support one another is to build resilience,
For in solidarity, there is strength,
In solidarity, there is change,
To lift one is to lift all, to empower one is to empower many.

10. Confront the power that dehumanizes,
That sees people as numbers, as resources,
For every life is a story, every person a universe,
To dehumanize is to deny the essence of humanity,
But to see the person, to see the soul,
Is to recognize the intrinsic value of each being,
To create a world where all are seen, all are valued,
For in valuing the human,
We create a world of compassion, of justice.

11. To confront power is to embrace vulnerability,
For to stand against the tide is to expose oneself,
To the criticism, the judgment, the backlash,
But vulnerability is not weakness; it is strength,
For it takes courage to be open, to be real,
To show the world not just the facade,
But the heart, the wounds, the dreams,
For in vulnerability, there is authenticity,

And in authenticity, there is the power to connect.

12. The world is shaped by those who dare,
Dare to think differently, to speak boldly,
To challenge the norms, to question the rules,
For progress is not found in comfort,
But in the discomfort of change,
To disrupt the patterns, to break the cycles,
For it is in daring to defy,
That we carve new paths,
And in new paths, find new futures.

13. Confront the power that silences,
For silence is the ally of oppression,
To keep the voices quiet, the truths hidden,
But every voice has a right to be heard,
Every story a right to be told,
To speak is to resist, to resist is to exist,
For in the noise of voices united,
There is a power that cannot be ignored,
A call for change, a call for justice.

14. To achieve change is to inspire hope,
For hope is the light that guides in the dark,
The spark that ignites action,
In the face of despair, in the face of doubt,
To believe that a better world is possible,
To act as if it is inevitable,
For hope is not passive, it is active,
A force that drives us forward,
Towards a future that is fair, that is just.

15. The power of change is in the hands of the many,
Not the few, for it is the collective,
The shared vision, the shared struggle,
That brings about transformation,
To empower others is to empower oneself,
To lift others is to rise higher,

For the success of one is the success of all,
To create a world where all can thrive,
For in the many, there is power, there is change.

16. Confront the power that corrupts,
For corruption is a poison, a disease,
It rots the soul, it decays the mind,
To be ethical, to be just,
Is to live in a way that honors others,
To act not out of greed, but out of care,
For it is integrity that builds,
And corruption that destroys,
To choose the path of integrity,
Is to choose the path of life.

17. The change we seek begins within,
For to change the world, we must first change ourselves,
To be the example, to be the light,
To live the values we wish to see,
For in our actions, in our choices,
We set the standard, we set the tone,
To act with kindness, with empathy,
To live with purpose, with meaning,
For in the change within, there is the change without.

18. Challenge the power that fears difference,
For it is in difference that we find innovation,
In diversity, we find strength,
To embrace the other, to embrace the unknown,
For fear is the barrier, the wall,
But love is the bridge, the connection,
To see beyond the surface,
To the essence, the core,
For in embracing difference, we find unity, we find strength.

19. To create change is to be persistent,
For change is not instant, but gradual,
A process of steps, of stages,

To be patient, to be diligent,
For every effort, every action counts,
To not be discouraged by setbacks,
But to learn, to adapt, to continue,
For it is in persistence, that we find success,
In persistence, that we find change.

20. The power of change is in the imagination,
To see the world not just as it is,
But as it could be, as it should be,
To dream of a society where all are equal,
Where justice is the norm, not the exception,
For it is imagination that breaks the chains,
That opens the doors to new possibilities,
To create a future that is bright,
A future that is free,
For in imagination, there is the seed of reality,
In imagination, there is the birth of change.

21. Confront the power that seeks to control thought,
For freedom of mind is the foundation of liberty,
To think freely is to live fully,
To question, to wonder, to explore,
For it is in the realm of ideas,
That revolutions are born,
To embrace critical thinking,
To value knowledge, to pursue wisdom,
For in the liberation of the mind, there is the birth of progress.

22. To create change is to be resilient,
For the path of transformation is not smooth,
It is filled with obstacles, with resistance,
But resilience is the ability to endure,
To rise after each fall, to continue after each setback,
For it is not the absence of struggle,
But the response to it, that defines us,
To persist, to push forward,
For in resilience, there is the power to overcome.

23. The power to change lies in the heart,
In the capacity to love, to care deeply,
For love is the force that heals,
That bridges divides, that unites,
To act out of love is to act selflessly,
To see beyond oneself, to the needs of others,
For in love, there is the power to transform,
To create a world where all are cherished,
For in the heart, there is the seed of change.

24. Confront the power that ignores the earth,
For the earth is our home, our mother,
To exploit it is to harm ourselves,
To care for it is to care for all life,
For in the balance of nature, there is wisdom,
A harmony that sustains, that nurtures,
To live in harmony with the earth,
To respect its limits, to honor its gifts,
For in caring for the earth, we care for our future.

25. The power of change is in the community,
In the coming together of people,
With shared values, with shared goals,
For a community united is a force unstoppable,
To work together, to support each other,
To build a society that is fair, that is just,
For it is in the community,
That we find belonging, that we find strength,
To create a world where all can thrive.

26. To create change is to be aware of privilege,
To recognize the advantages one holds,
And to use them for the benefit of others,
For privilege is not a right, but a responsibility,
To lift those who are marginalized,
To amplify the voices that are silenced,
For in using privilege for good,

There is the power to balance,
To create a society of equals, a society of justice.

27. Confront the power that thrives on ignorance,
For ignorance is the root of fear,
And fear is the tool of control,
To educate is to liberate,
To inform is to empower,
For knowledge is the light that dispels darkness,
To seek truth, to value education,
For in enlightenment, there is freedom,
In freedom, there is the power to choose.

28. The power to create change is in the courage to act,
To take the first step, to lead by example,
For action speaks louder than words,
To not just talk of change, but to be change,
For it is in the doing, that we find purpose,
To be the catalyst, to be the spark,
For in action, there is movement,
In movement, there is transformation,
For in the courage to act, there is the power to inspire.

29. Confront the power that isolates,
For isolation breeds loneliness, breeds fear,
To connect is to build, to reach out is to heal,
For in connection, there is strength,
To foster relationships, to build networks,
For it is in the bonds of friendship,
That we find support, that we find community,
To live not in isolation, but in connection,
For in togetherness, there is the power to change.

30. To create change is to have faith,
Not blind faith, but faith in humanity,
In the goodness of people, in the possibility of progress,
For cynicism is the enemy of action,
To believe that a better world is possible,

Is to work towards it, to fight for it,
For faith is the foundation of hope,
And hope is the foundation of change,
For in believing, there is the power to achieve.

31. Confront the power that thrives on inequality,
For inequality is a wound that festers,
A barrier that divides, that oppresses,
To create a world where everyone has a chance,
Where opportunity is not a privilege, but a right,
To break down the walls that separate,
To build bridges of understanding, of fairness,
For in equality, there is peace,
And in peace, there is the foundation of a just society.

32. The power of change lies in the hands of the youth,
For they are the visionaries, the dreamers,
Unburdened by the constraints of the past,
To see the world with fresh eyes,
To question the old, to seek the new,
For the future is theirs to shape,
To encourage, to inspire, to guide,
For in the youth, there is energy,
And in their energy, there is the promise of a better world.

33. To create change is to embrace innovation,
To think outside the box, to challenge the norm,
For progress is not found in tradition,
But in the new ideas, the bold solutions,
To take risks, to explore the unknown,
For it is in the unknown that we find discovery,
To foster creativity, to value imagination,
For in innovation, there is the power to transform,
And in transformation, there is the key to the future.

Unremarkable 6, 2024

Book 5

Living with Purpose and Clarity

1. To live with purpose is to live intentionally,
To move through life with direction,
Not swayed by the fleeting desires of the moment,
But guided by a deeper sense of meaning,
For purpose is not found in the pursuit of pleasure,
But in the pursuit of what is right, what is good,
To know why you rise each day,
To have a cause that drives you forward,
For in purpose, there is fulfillment, there is peace.

2. Clarity is the gift of a focused mind,
To see the world without distortion,
To cut through the noise, the distractions,
To understand what truly matters,
For a life lived with clarity is a life of intention,
To be mindful of each action, each choice,
To see the path ahead not as a blur,
But as a clear road, a journey well-defined,
For in clarity, there is direction, there is strength.

3. Purpose is the compass that guides the soul,
To have a reason, a why,
For without purpose, life is aimless,
A drift on the sea of uncertainty,
But with purpose, there is a destination,
A goal that gives meaning to each step,
To know what you seek, what you strive for,
To have a mission that gives life depth,
For in purpose, there is motivation, there is drive.

4. To live with clarity is to live simply,
To strip away the excess, the unnecessary,

76

To focus on what is essential,
To value quality over quantity,
For a cluttered life is a confused life,
But a simple life is a clear life,
To know what you need, what you value,
To live with less, but to live with more meaning,
For in simplicity, there is clarity, there is joy.

5. Purpose is found in the service of others,
To use your talents, your strengths,
Not just for yourself, but for the good of all,
For in giving, there is receiving,
In serving, there is fulfillment,
To know that your life makes a difference,
That your actions matter,
For in purpose, there is connection, there is love.

6. Clarity is the result of self-reflection,
To take time to know oneself,
To understand one's desires, one's fears,
For self-knowledge is the foundation of clarity,
To see oneself honestly, without illusion,
To accept both strengths and weaknesses,
For in self-awareness, there is wisdom,
And in wisdom, there is clarity, there is peace.

7. To live with purpose is to live with passion,
To find what sets your soul on fire,
What makes you feel alive,
For passion is the fuel of purpose,
The energy that drives you forward,
To have a cause, a dream that ignites you,
To live each day with enthusiasm,
For in passion, there is life, there is joy.

8. Clarity is found in the present moment,
To be fully here, fully now,
Not lost in the regrets of the past,

Or the anxieties of the future,
To see the beauty, the opportunity,
That exists in each breath, each heartbeat,
For in the present, there is clarity,
In clarity, there is freedom, there is peace.

9. Purpose is not a destination, but a journey,
A path that unfolds with each step,
To live with purpose is to live with curiosity,
To seek, to explore, to discover,
For purpose is not fixed, but evolves,
With each experience, each lesson learned,
To be open to change, to growth,
For in the journey, there is discovery,
In discovery, there is purpose, there is life.

10. Clarity comes from letting go,
Of what no longer serves,
Of the attachments that bind,
For freedom is found in release,
To let go of the need to control,
To accept, to flow, to trust,
For in letting go, there is clarity,
In clarity, there is serenity, there is grace.

11. To live with purpose is to live with integrity,
To be true to oneself, to one's values,
For a life of purpose is a life of honor,
To act with honesty, with sincerity,
To keep one's word, to follow through,
For in integrity, there is trust,
In trust, there is purpose, there is respect.

12. Clarity is found in stillness,
In the quiet moments of reflection,
To take time to pause, to breathe,
For in the stillness, there is space,
To think, to feel, to understand,

To find the answers, the insight,
For in stillness, there is clarity,
In clarity, there is insight, there is wisdom.

13. Purpose is the flame that lights the way,
A beacon in the darkness, a guide in the fog,
To hold onto purpose is to hold onto hope,
For in purpose, there is light, there is direction,
To walk the path with confidence,
Knowing that each step is part of a greater whole,
For purpose is the thread that weaves meaning,
Into the fabric of life, into the journey of the soul.

14. Clarity is found in the alignment of mind and heart,
To think with reason, to feel with compassion,
For clarity is not cold, but warm,
A balance of logic and love,
To see with the eyes of understanding,
To hear with the ears of empathy,
For in this balance, there is clarity,
And in clarity, there is a deeper understanding of life.

15. To live with purpose is to live with courage,
To face the challenges, the obstacles,
Not with fear, but with determination,
For purpose gives strength, gives resilience,
To stand firm in the storm,
To continue in the face of doubt,
For in courage, there is purpose,
And in purpose, there is the will to endure.

16. Clarity is the antidote to confusion,
To see through the haze, the uncertainty,
To understand what is real, what is true,
For clarity cuts through the illusion,
To reveal the essence, the core,
To know what matters, what is important,
For in clarity, there is truth,

And in truth, there is the foundation of wisdom.

17. Purpose is the bridge between dreams and reality,
To turn vision into action,
To take the steps, to make the moves,
For purpose is not just about thinking,
But about doing, about being,
To make the dream tangible,
To bring the vision to life,
For in action, there is purpose,
And in purpose, there is the manifestation of dreams.

18. Clarity is the art of discernment,
To separate the noise from the signal,
To focus on what is meaningful,
To let go of what distracts,
For a clear mind is a sharp mind,
Able to see the path, to make the choice,
For in discernment, there is clarity,
And in clarity, there is the ability to decide.

19. To live with purpose is to live with a sense of legacy,
To know that your life leaves a mark,
That your actions ripple through time,
For purpose is not just for the present,
But for the future, for those who come after,
To live a life that inspires, that uplifts,
For in legacy, there is purpose,
And in purpose, there is the continuity of life.

20. Clarity is the space between thoughts,
The quiet that exists before the noise,
To find the silence, the stillness,
To rest in the calm, in the peace,
For clarity is not found in the rush,
But in the pause, in the breath,
To listen to the inner voice,
For in stillness, there is clarity,

And in clarity, there is the wisdom of the soul.

21. Purpose is the alignment of intention and action,
To not just desire, but to do,
To take steps that are consistent with beliefs,
For a life of purpose is a life of coherence,
Where what is thought, is said, is done,
To be whole, to be one,
For in alignment, there is purpose,
And in purpose, there is the fulfillment of life.

22. Clarity comes from living authentically,
To be true to oneself, to one's nature,
Not to wear masks, not to play roles,
But to be real, to be genuine,
For authenticity brings clarity,
A clear sense of who one is,
To live with integrity, to live with truth,
For in authenticity, there is clarity,
And in clarity, there is the essence of being.

23. To live with purpose is to embrace responsibility,
To understand the impact of one's actions,
To know that each choice matters,
For purpose is not about self, but about others,
To live for a cause greater than oneself,
To take on the burden, to bear the weight,
For in responsibility, there is purpose,
And in purpose, there is the strength to carry on.

24. Clarity is found in the acceptance of change,
To see life as fluid, as ever-evolving,
Not to cling to the past, but to flow with the present,
For change is the nature of life,
To adapt, to adjust, to grow,
For in acceptance, there is clarity,
And in clarity, there is the freedom to live.

25. Purpose is the courage to stand alone,
When the world does not understand,
To hold to one's beliefs, to one's values,
For purpose is not about popularity,
But about conviction, about truth,
To be a voice of reason, a beacon of light,
For in standing alone, there is purpose,
And in purpose, there is the power to inspire.

26. Clarity comes from knowing your limits,
To recognize where you end and the world begins,
To understand your strengths and embrace your weaknesses,
For in acknowledging boundaries, there is wisdom,
Not as a sign of weakness, but as a measure of truth,
To know when to push forward and when to hold back,
For in knowing one's limits, there is clarity,
And in clarity, there is the freedom to act with wisdom and
grace.

27. Clarity is born from purpose-driven silence,
The intentional pause before action,
To contemplate not just the next step,
But the why behind the journey,
For silence is not absence, but presence,
A space to listen to the inner voice,
To align the heart with the mind's intent,
For in purpose-driven silence, there is clarity,
And in clarity, the wisdom to move forward with intention.

Unremarkable 7, 2024

Book 6

Inner Strength and Collective Action

1. Inner strength is forged in the fires of adversity,
Not in ease or comfort, but in challenge,
To face each struggle not as an obstacle,
But as a forge, a place of growth,
For strength is not just of the body,
But of the mind, of the spirit,
To stand firm in the face of oppression,
To remain unbroken by the weight of injustice,
For in resilience, there is the seed of change.

2. Collective action begins with the recognition,
That no one is free until all are free,
To see the chains that bind others,
As chains that bind us all,
For in the fight against patriarchy,
In the struggle against bigotry,
We stand not just for ourselves,
But for each other,
For in unity, there is power; in solidarity, strength.

3. The power of the individual lies not in isolation,
But in connection, in community,
For we are stronger together,
Bound by common cause,
To challenge the forces of capitalism,
That seeks to divide, to conquer,
For the greed of a few,
Is the suffering of many,
To stand together is to reclaim our humanity.

4. Inner strength is the courage to be oneself,

To not conform to the expectations of others,
To define success not by wealth or status,
But by integrity, by authenticity,
For the true measure of a person,
Is not in what they have, but who they are,
To live a life of truth,
To be a beacon of light,
For in authenticity, there is strength, in strength, change.

5. Collective action is the voice of the many,
Rising against the silence of oppression,
To speak out against injustice,
To be the voice of the voiceless,
For silence is the ally of the oppressor,
But the roar of the collective,
Is a force that cannot be silenced,
To march, to protest, to demand,
For in action, there is power, in power, liberation.

6. The strength of the spirit is in compassion,
To feel for others, to care deeply,
To see beyond oneself, to the suffering of others,
For compassion is not a weakness,
But a source of strength, a call to action,
To heal, to help, to support,
For in compassion, there is unity,
In unity, there is the power to change,
To build a world where all are cared for.

7. Collective action is the refusal to accept,
The world as it is,
To envision a world as it could be,
Where patriarchy does not dictate,
Where bigotry does not divide,
Where capitalism does not exploit,
To dream of a society of equals,
To work towards a future of fairness,
For in dreaming, there is hope, in hope, action.

8. Inner strength is the resolve to keep going,
Even when the path is hard,
To not be discouraged by setbacks,
To not be defeated by failure,
For strength is not in never falling,
But in always rising,
To persist, to endure,
For in persistence, there is power,
And in power, there is the catalyst for change.

9. Collective action is the recognition,
That every voice matters, every action counts,
To see each person as part of the whole,
To value each contribution,
For the strength of the collective,
Is in its diversity, in its inclusivity,
To build a movement that is broad,
That is inclusive, that is just,
For in inclusion, there is strength, in strength, victory.

10. The strength to resist lies in self-awareness,
To know oneself, to understand one's values,
To act not out of anger, but out of principle,
For the fight against injustice,
Is a fight for the soul,
To remain true to oneself,
To stand firm in one's beliefs,
For in self-awareness, there is clarity,
And in clarity, the resolve to resist.

11. Collective action is a tapestry,
Woven from the threads of many lives,
To see the beauty in each strand,
To honor each person's story,
For a movement is not a monolith,
But a mosaic, a chorus of voices,
To celebrate the differences,

To find strength in diversity,
For in the tapestry, there is beauty, in beauty, unity.

12. Inner strength is the ability to adapt,
To change, to grow, to evolve,
To not be rigid, but to be flexible,
For strength is not in being unyielding,
But in being resilient,
To bend but not break,
To learn, to adapt, to thrive,
For in adaptation, there is survival,
And in survival, the foundation for change.

13. Inner strength is found in the quiet moments,
In the reflection, the contemplation,
To know one's thoughts, one's heart,
To find peace in solitude,
For strength is not always loud,
Sometimes it is the calm in the storm,
To find solace in one's own company,
To be content with oneself,
For in quiet, there is power, and in power, peace.

14. Collective action is fueled by empathy,
The ability to see the world through another's eyes,
To feel the pain, the joy, the hope,
Of those who are different,
For empathy bridges divides,
It connects us in our shared humanity,
To act not just for oneself,
But for the betterment of all,
For in empathy, there is connection; in connection, change.

15. The strength to endure comes from purpose,
To know why you fight, why you resist,
For a life without purpose is a life without direction,
To have a cause that is greater than oneself,
To work towards a vision, a dream,

For purpose gives meaning to struggle,
It gives hope to the weary,
To endure is to believe,
For in purpose, there is hope, and in hope, resilience.

16. Collective action requires courage,
The bravery to stand up, to speak out,
Even when it is dangerous,
For courage is not the absence of fear,
But the decision to act in spite of it,
To face the unknown, to challenge the status quo,
For in courage, there is change,
And in change, there is the possibility of a better world.

17. Inner strength is the ability to forgive,
To let go of anger, of resentment,
For forgiveness is not weakness,
It is the strength to move forward,
To heal, to grow, to find peace,
For holding onto anger is a burden,
But forgiveness is liberation,
To be free of the past,
For in forgiveness, there is freedom, and in freedom, healing.

18. Collective action is the art of listening,
To hear the voices of those who are often ignored,
To value the perspectives, the experiences,
Of those who are different,
For listening is the first step to understanding,
And understanding is the first step to unity,
To build a movement that is inclusive,
That honors each voice,
For in listening, there is respect, and in respect, solidarity.

19. The strength to resist is the strength to hope,
To believe that change is possible,
Even when it seems distant,
For hope is the light in the darkness,

The guide in the uncertainty,
To hold onto hope is to hold onto life,
To see the possibility in the impossible,
For in hope, there is strength, and in strength, action.

20. Collective action is rooted in justice,
The desire to see fairness, to see equality,
To challenge the systems that oppress,
To fight for those who cannot fight for themselves,
For justice is not just a word,
It is a call to action, a demand for change,
To see the world not as it is,
But as it should be,
For in justice, there is righteousness, and in righteousness,
power.

21. Inner strength is the ability to remain humble,
To not let power corrupt, to not let success inflate,
To remember where you come from,
To stay grounded in your values,
For humility is the foundation of strength,
To lead not with ego, but with heart,
To serve, not to dominate,
For in humility, there is wisdom, and in wisdom, guidance.

22. Collective action is the spark of revolution,
The moment when people come together,
To demand change, to demand better,
For revolution is not just in the streets,
It is in the hearts, the minds,
To see the possibility of a different world,
To work together to make it a reality,
For in revolution, there is the birth of new beginnings.

23. The strength to change lies in adaptability,
To be open to new ideas, new ways,
For change is the only constant,
To resist it is to be left behind,

But to embrace it is to grow,
To evolve, to become,
For adaptability is not a sign of weakness,
But a sign of strength,
For in change, there is growth, and in growth, life.

24. Collective action is a journey,
Not a destination,
To see each step, each action,
As part of a greater whole,
For the path to change is long,
It is not easy, but it is worth it,
To be patient, to be persistent,
To know that each effort counts,
For in the journey, there is purpose, and in purpose, fulfillment.

25. Inner strength is the commitment to truth,
To see the world as it is,
Not as we wish it to be,
To speak truth, even when it is difficult,
For truth is the foundation of trust,
And trust is the foundation of action,
To live with integrity,
To be honest, to be real,
For in truth, there is power, and in power, respect.

26. Collective action is the building of bridges,
To connect communities, to connect causes,
For division is the tool of oppression,
But unity is the tool of liberation,
To see beyond the differences,
To find the common ground,
For in unity, there is strength,
And in strength, the power to change the world.

Unremarkable 8, 2024

Book 7

Navigating the World with Wisdom and Courage

1. Wisdom is the compass that guides the soul,
Not found in books alone, but in life lived,
To see the world as it is, not as we wish,
To understand the forces that shape our paths,
For true wisdom challenges the status quo,
Questions the norms that go unexamined,
To navigate with eyes wide open,
To see beyond the surface,
For in wisdom, there is the power to discern.

2. Curiosity is the flame that lights the way,
A hunger for knowledge, a thirst for truth,
To ask the questions that others avoid,
To explore the unknown, the unfamiliar,
For curiosity is not complacent,
It does not accept things as they are,
But seeks to understand, to learn,
For in curiosity, there is discovery,
And in discovery, there is the seed of change.

3. To navigate the world with wisdom,
Is to see the systems that bind us,
The chains of patriarchy that restrict,
The shadows of bigotry that divide,
To challenge the structures that oppress,
To stand against the forces that exploit,
For wisdom is not passive, but active,
A call to question, to resist,
For in challenging power, there is liberation.

4. Curiosity is the courage to explore,
To step beyond the known, the comfortable,

To venture into new ideas, new perspectives,
For the world is vast, and so is knowledge,
To be open to different ways of seeing,
To embrace the richness of diversity,
For in diversity, there is strength,
In new perspectives, there is growth,
For in curiosity, there is the expansion of the mind.

5. Wisdom is found in the balance,
To know when to act, and when to wait,
To see the bigger picture, the long-term view,
For wisdom is not rushed, but thoughtful,
To weigh the options, to consider the outcomes,
For every choice has its consequence,
To act with intention, with foresight,
For in wisdom, there is clarity,
And in clarity, there is purpose.

6. Curiosity is the antidote to ignorance,
To seek knowledge for its own sake,
Not for power, not for gain,
But to understand, to connect,
For the world is a puzzle,
And each piece is a piece of the whole,
To see the connections, the patterns,
For in curiosity, there is understanding,
And in understanding, there is empathy.

7. To navigate the world with wisdom,
Is to value the voices of the marginalized,
To listen to those who are often silenced,
For wisdom is not found in echo chambers,
But in the voices of the diverse,
To see the world from different angles,
For every perspective adds to the whole,
To challenge the dominance of a single view,
For in diversity, there is the richness of wisdom.

8. Curiosity is the willingness to be wrong,
To admit that one does not know,
For there is no shame in ignorance,
Only in the refusal to learn,
To be open to new information,
To change one's mind, to grow,
For the wise are not rigid, but flexible,
To adapt, to evolve,
For in curiosity, there is the humility to learn.

9. Wisdom is the strength to stand alone,
To hold to one's convictions,
Even when they are unpopular,
For wisdom is not about agreement,
But about truth, about justice,
To be a voice of reason in a world of noise,
To stand for what is right,
For in wisdom, there is courage,
And in courage, there is the power to change.

10. Curiosity is the drive to innovate,
To see problems as opportunities,
To seek solutions that are new, that are bold,
For the world is in constant change,
And so must be our thinking,
To not be bound by tradition,
But to seek better ways,
For in curiosity, there is innovation,
And in innovation, there is the potential for a better world.

11. To navigate the world with wisdom,
Is to see beyond the individual,
To understand the collective, the community,
For wisdom knows that we are all connected,
That the actions of one affect the many,
To act not just for oneself,
But for the greater good,
For in wisdom, there is the recognition of our shared humanity.

12. Curiosity is the spirit of adventure,
To explore the world with open eyes,
To see the beauty, the wonder,
In the ordinary, in the everyday,
For the world is full of miracles,
Waiting to be discovered,
To live with a sense of awe, of wonder,
For in curiosity, there is joy,
And in joy, there is the celebration of life.

13. Wisdom is the pursuit of justice,
To see the inequalities, the injustices,
To not turn a blind eye,
But to take action, to make a difference,
For wisdom is not passive, but engaged,
To be a force for good,
To challenge the status quo,
For in justice, there is peace,
And in peace, there is the foundation of a better world.

14. Curiosity is the openness to others,
To seek out different cultures, different ways,
To learn from those who are different,
For every culture has its wisdom,
To build bridges, not walls,
To see the humanity in each person,
For in curiosity, there is respect,
And in respect, there is the foundation of community.

15. To navigate the world with wisdom,
Is to live with integrity,
To be true to oneself, to one's values,
For wisdom is not just about knowledge,
But about how one lives,
To be consistent, to be honest,
To act with honor,
For in wisdom, there is integrity,

And in integrity, there is the foundation of trust.

16. Wisdom is in the quiet strength,
To listen more than to speak,
To understand rather than to judge,
For wisdom does not shout, it whispers,
Guiding with gentle hands,
To see the value in every life,
To act with compassion, with kindness,
For in listening, there is wisdom,
And in understanding, there is the foundation for unity.

17. Curiosity is the courage to challenge,
To question the narratives that bind us,
The myths of supremacy, the lies of hierarchy,
For curiosity does not accept without proof,
It probes, it seeks, it finds,
To unearth the truths buried beneath the surface,
For in questioning, there is freedom,
And in freedom, there is the liberation of the mind.

18. To navigate the world with wisdom,
Is to recognize the power of the collective,
To know that no one succeeds alone,
To see the strength in community, in collaboration,
For wisdom values the many, not the few,
To uplift, to support, to empower,
For in unity, there is resilience,
And in resilience, there is the power to endure.

19. Curiosity is the love of learning,
To never be satisfied with what one knows,
To always seek more, to go deeper,
For the world is a vast ocean of knowledge,
And we are but explorers,
To dive into the depths,
To bring forth the treasures of understanding,
For in learning, there is growth,

And in growth, there is the expansion of the soul.

20. Wisdom is the patience to wait,
To not rush into decisions,
But to consider, to reflect,
For haste often leads to regret,
But patience allows for clarity,
To see the full picture, to understand the consequences,
For in patience, there is wisdom,
And in wisdom, there is the power to choose wisely.

21. Curiosity is the antidote to apathy,
To care about the world, about others,
To be engaged, to be involved,
For apathy is the death of the soul,
But curiosity breathes life,
To be passionate, to be active,
For in caring, there is purpose,
And in purpose, there is the drive to make a difference.

22. To navigate the world with wisdom,
Is to value justice over convenience,
To take the harder road, the road less traveled,
For wisdom knows that what is easy is not always right,
To stand up for what is just,
Even when it is difficult,
For in justice, there is righteousness,
And in righteousness, there is the foundation for peace.

23. Curiosity is the joy of exploration,
To see the world with new eyes,
To find the extraordinary in the ordinary,
For the world is full of wonders,
For those who are willing to look,
To be amazed, to be inspired,
For in exploration, there is joy,
And in joy, there is the celebration of life.

24. Wisdom is the art of letting go,
To release what no longer serves,
To not hold onto the past,
But to embrace the present,
For holding on is to be weighed down,
But letting go is to be free,
To move forward, to grow,
For in letting go, there is peace,
And in peace, there is the freedom to live fully.

25. Curiosity is the resistance to complacency,
To not settle for what is,
But to seek what could be,
For complacency breeds stagnation,
But curiosity breeds innovation,
To strive for better, to aim higher,
For in resistance, there is progress,
And in progress, there is the path to a better world.

26. To navigate the world with wisdom,
Is to find strength in vulnerability,
To not hide one's flaws,
But to embrace them,
For vulnerability is not weakness,
It is the courage to be real,
To be open, to be honest,
For in vulnerability, there is connection,
And in connection, there is the power to heal.

27. Curiosity is the drive to make the invisible visible,
To bring to light what is hidden,
To speak the truths that are often silenced,
For there is power in knowledge,
And even more in its revelation,
To challenge the secrecy that protects the powerful,
For in truth, there is justice,
And in justice, there is the foundation for change.

Unremarkable 9, 2024

Book 8

Creating a Compassionate Future

1. Compassion is the foundation of a just world,
To see the suffering of others as our own,
To act not out of self-interest,
But out of a deep sense of empathy,
For a compassionate heart knows no boundaries,
It transcends race, gender, class,
To embrace all of humanity,
For in compassion, there is the seed of justice,
And in justice, the hope for a better world.

2. A compassionate future begins with equity,
To recognize the imbalances that exist,
To work towards a world where opportunity is shared,
Where privilege does not dictate destiny,
For true equality is not just in words,
But in actions, in policies, in laws,
To create a society where all can thrive,
For in equity, there is fairness,
And in fairness, the promise of a compassionate future.

3. Compassion is not passive; it is active,
To be moved by the plight of others,
To take action to alleviate suffering,
For compassion without action is mere sentiment,
But compassion with action is transformative,
To feed the hungry, to shelter the homeless,
To fight for the rights of the marginalized,
For in action, there is change,
And in change, the creation of a compassionate world.

4. A compassionate future values diversity,
To see the richness in different cultures,

100

The beauty in different perspectives,
For diversity is not a threat, but a strength,
To build a world where all voices are heard,
Where all stories are told,
For in diversity, there is resilience,
And in resilience, the capacity to grow,
To create a future where all are respected.

5. Compassion is the courage to challenge power,
To stand up against the systems that oppress,
To speak out against the injustices of patriarchy,
To dismantle the structures of bigotry,
For a compassionate heart cannot remain silent,
It must act, it must resist,
For in resistance, there is hope,
And in hope, the birth of a compassionate society.

6. A compassionate future is built on solidarity,
To stand with those who are oppressed,
To fight alongside those who are marginalized,
For in solidarity, there is strength,
To see the struggles of others as our own,
To work together for a common cause,
For in unity, there is power,
And in power, the ability to create change,
To build a world where all are free.

7. Compassion is the recognition of shared humanity,
To see beyond the labels, the divisions,
To recognize that we are all connected,
For the pain of one is the pain of all,
To act with kindness, with understanding,
For in compassion, there is the bond of humanity,
And in humanity, the call for a compassionate future.

8. A compassionate future rejects greed,
To see wealth not as a measure of success,
But as a means to do good, to uplift others,

For capitalism without compassion is exploitation,
To build a system that values people over profit,
To create a world where resources are shared,
For in sharing, there is abundance,
And in abundance, the ability to care for all.

9. Compassion is the commitment to education,
To teach the next generation the values of empathy,
The importance of justice, the power of kindness,
For education is the foundation of a compassionate society,
To nurture minds that are open, that are curious,
To build a future where ignorance does not breed hate,
For in education, there is understanding,
And in understanding, the capacity for compassion.

10. A compassionate future honors the earth,
To see the environment not as a resource to exploit,
But as a home to be cared for, to be protected,
For the health of the earth is the health of all,
To live in harmony with nature,
To respect the limits of the land,
For in sustainability, there is life,
And in life, the possibility of a compassionate world.

11. Compassion is the strength to forgive,
To let go of past wrongs, to heal wounds,
For forgiveness is not about forgetting,
But about moving forward,
To build bridges, to create understanding,
For in forgiveness, there is healing,
And in healing, the foundation for a compassionate future.

12. A compassionate future is built on transparency,
To have systems that are open, that are just,
To hold those in power accountable,
For secrecy breeds corruption,
But transparency fosters trust,
To have leaders who serve, not dominate,

For in transparency, there is accountability,
And in accountability, the foundation for justice.

13. Compassion is the embrace of vulnerability,
To show weakness, to show need,
For vulnerability is not a sign of failure,
But a sign of humanity,
To connect with others in our shared struggles,
For in vulnerability, there is strength,
And in strength, the capacity to create a compassionate society.

14. A compassionate future nurtures creativity,
To see the arts as a vital part of life,
To value imagination, innovation, expression,
For creativity is the language of the soul,
To support artists, to encourage thinkers,
For in creativity, there is the ability to inspire,
And in inspiration, the power to transform,
To create a future that is vibrant, that is alive.

15. Compassion is the practice of humility,
To know that no one has all the answers,
To be open to learning, to growing,
For humility is the recognition of our limitations,
To seek wisdom from others, to value collaboration,
For in humility, there is wisdom,
And in wisdom, the foundation for a compassionate future.

16. A compassionate future is rooted in kindness,
To treat others with gentleness, with care,
To see each person as valuable, as worthy,
For kindness costs nothing, but means everything,
To create a world where compassion is the norm,
Not the exception, where care is a given,
For in kindness, there is healing,
And in healing, the foundation for peace.

17. Compassion is the rejection of fear,

To not be ruled by the fear of the other,
To see beyond differences to the shared human experience,
For fear is the tool of oppression,
But love is the force of liberation,
To choose love over fear, to choose unity over division,
For in love, there is power,
And in power, the ability to transform.

18. A compassionate future is built on generosity,
To give freely, without expectation,
To share what one has, to uplift those in need,
For generosity is the heart of community,
To create a world where resources are abundant,
Not because of what is taken, but because of what is given,
For in giving, there is joy,
And in joy, the creation of a compassionate society.

19. Compassion is the practice of patience,
To understand that change takes time,
To be patient with others, and with oneself,
For growth is a process, not an event,
To nurture, to support, to guide,
For in patience, there is understanding,
And in understanding, the capacity to build a better world.

20. A compassionate future values mental health,
To see the importance of well-being,
To support those who struggle,
For mental health is as vital as physical health,
To break the stigma, to open the dialogue,
To create a society where everyone is cared for,
For in caring for the mind, there is the foundation for a thriving
community.

21. Compassion is the embrace of joy,
To find happiness in the simple things,
To celebrate life, to laugh, to love,
For joy is a form of resistance,

To find light in the darkest of times,
To create a world where joy is abundant,
For in joy, there is hope,
And in hope, the resilience to endure.

22. A compassionate future rejects violence,
To see peace not as the absence of war,
But as the presence of justice,
To resolve conflict through dialogue,
To choose negotiation over force,
For true strength is found in peace,
To create a world where violence is not the answer,
For in peace, there is security,
And in security, the foundation for a compassionate society.

23. Compassion is the strength to stand up,
To speak out against wrongs,
To be a voice for those who cannot speak,
For silence in the face of injustice is complicity,
To take a stand, to take action,
For in standing up, there is courage,
And in courage, the power to change.

24. A compassionate future is inclusive,
To see all people as part of the whole,
To value each individual,
For a society that excludes, destroys,
But a society that includes, thrives,
To build a world where all are welcome,
Where all are valued,
For in inclusion, there is community,
And in community, the strength to build a compassionate future.

25. Compassion is the commitment to truth,
To seek honesty, to value transparency,
For lies are the roots of oppression,
But truth is the light that dispels darkness,

To speak truth, even when it is hard,
To live truth, even when it is costly,
For in truth, there is freedom,
And in freedom, the creation of a just world.

26. A compassionate future respects autonomy,
To honor the right of each person to choose,
To make decisions about their own lives,
For autonomy is the essence of dignity,
To support the freedom of thought,
The freedom of expression,
For in autonomy, there is respect,
And in respect, the foundation for peace.

27. Compassion is the recognition of interdependence,
To see that we are all connected,
That our actions affect others,
To live with a sense of responsibility,
For the well-being of all,
To act not just for oneself,
But for the greater good,
For in interdependence, there is community,
And in community, the capacity to create a compassionate
world.

28. A compassionate future embraces the youth,
To nurture the next generation,
To teach them the values of empathy, of justice,
For the future belongs to them,
To give them the tools, the knowledge,
To build a world that is fair, that is kind,
For in the youth, there is the promise of tomorrow,
And in that promise, the hope for a better world.

Unremarkable 10, 2024

Book 9

Building Bridges, Breaking Barriers

1. Building bridges begins with listening,
To hear the stories of those we do not know,
To understand the struggles that are not our own,
For in listening, there is connection,
A way to see the world through different eyes,
To break the silence that divides us,
For in hearing each other, we build the foundation,
For a bridge that spans the divides of fear,
A connection that is built on understanding.

2. Breaking barriers starts with questioning,
To challenge the beliefs that keep us apart,
The prejudices that are handed down,
For barriers are built on ignorance,
On the refusal to see beyond the surface,
To question is to seek truth,
To dismantle the walls that are built on lies,
For in questioning, there is enlightenment,
And in enlightenment, the freedom to unite.

3. Building bridges is an act of courage,
To reach out across the chasms of difference,
To extend a hand to those unlike ourselves,
For courage is not the absence of fear,
But the decision to act in spite of it,
To forge connections that are strong,
To create pathways of understanding,
For in courage, there is the strength to build,
And in building, the possibility of a united world.

4. Breaking barriers requires honesty,
To face the truths we'd rather avoid,

To acknowledge the privileges we hold,
For honesty is the light that reveals,
The structures that keep us apart,
To be honest is to be vulnerable,
To admit that we do not know everything,
For in honesty, there is growth,
And in growth, the power to overcome.

5. Building bridges means embracing diversity,
To see the beauty in our differences,
To celebrate the variety of human experience,
For diversity is not a threat, but a gift,
A source of strength, of resilience,
To create a world where all are welcome,
Where all are valued,
For in diversity, there is richness,
And in richness, the capacity to thrive.

6. Breaking barriers is about empowerment,
To lift up those who have been pushed down,
To give voice to those who have been silenced,
For empowerment is the key to liberation,
To ensure that all have the power to speak,
To make their voices heard,
For in empowerment, there is freedom,
And in freedom, the ability to create change.

7. Building bridges is an act of empathy,
To feel the pain of another as our own,
To share in the joys and sorrows of others,
For empathy is the glue that binds,
The connection that turns strangers into friends,
To create a world where compassion rules,
Where kindness is the norm,
For in empathy, there is unity,
And in unity, the strength to endure.

8. Breaking barriers means standing up,

Against the forces that divide,
The voices that preach hate and exclusion,
For to break a barrier is to challenge power,
To confront the systems that oppress,
To fight for a world that is just,
Where all are treated with dignity,
For in standing up, there is resistance,
And in resistance, the power to dismantle.

9. Building bridges is about common ground,
To find the things that unite us,
The shared hopes, the shared dreams,
For common ground is the foundation of peace,
To see beyond the differences,
To the humanity that connects us all,
To work together for a common cause,
For in common ground, there is solidarity,
And in solidarity, the promise of a better future.

10. Breaking barriers is an ongoing struggle,
For each generation must fight anew,
To challenge the injustices of their time,
For barriers are persistent,
They adapt, they evolve,
To break them requires vigilance,
To stay committed to the cause,
For in struggle, there is perseverance,
And in perseverance, the path to freedom.

11. Building bridges requires patience,
To understand that change takes time,
That relationships are built slowly,
For patience is the key to lasting connections,
To be willing to invest in the long term,
To see the value in each small step,
For in patience, there is stability,
And in stability, the power to endure.

12. Breaking barriers means challenging norms,
To question the way things have always been,
To imagine new ways of being,
For norms are the silent barriers,
The unspoken rules that confine,
To challenge them is to seek liberation,
To create a world where all can thrive,
For in challenging norms, there is innovation,
And in innovation, the potential for transformation.

13. Building bridges is about forgiveness,
To let go of past grievances,
To start anew, to build fresh,
For forgiveness is the path to reconciliation,
To heal the wounds that divide us,
To move forward together,
For in forgiveness, there is healing,
And in healing, the power to build anew.

14. Breaking barriers is an act of justice,
To right the wrongs of the past,
To ensure equality for all,
For justice is the foundation of peace,
To hold those in power accountable,
To fight for the rights of the marginalized,
For in justice, there is righteousness,
And in righteousness, the power to create a just world.

15. Building bridges is about love,
To love not just those who are like us,
But those who are different,
For love is the strongest bridge of all,
The connection that can withstand any storm,
To love unconditionally, to love boldly,
For in love, there is the essence of humanity,
And in humanity, the power to create a compassionate world.

16. Building bridges involves education,
To teach the truth of our shared history,
To uncover the narratives often silenced,
For education is a bridge to understanding,
To learn from the past to shape a better future,
To empower minds with knowledge,
For in education, there is enlightenment,
And in enlightenment, the capacity to create lasting change.

17. Breaking barriers means dismantling stereotypes,
To see beyond the labels, the assumptions,
To see each person as an individual,
For stereotypes are the chains that bind,
To challenge them is to seek freedom,
To create a world where people are seen,
For who they are, not what they are expected to be,
For in breaking stereotypes, there is liberation,
And in liberation, the possibility of a fair world.

18. Building bridges calls for inclusivity,
To ensure everyone has a seat at the table,
To value each voice, each perspective,
For inclusivity is the heart of democracy,
To create a society where everyone belongs,
Where everyone is heard,
For in inclusivity, there is strength,
And in strength, the power to build a united community.

19. Breaking barriers requires innovation,
To think outside the confines of tradition,
To imagine new ways of being,
For innovation is the tool of progress,
To challenge the status quo,
To find solutions that are bold, that are new,
For in innovation, there is potential,
And in potential, the opportunity to break free.

Unremarkable 11, 2024

Book 10

Nurturing Justice, Fostering Harmony

1. Justice is the bedrock of a fair society,
To seek what is right, to challenge what is wrong,
For justice is not just a word, but an action,
A commitment to equality, to fairness,
To ensure that all are treated with dignity,
To fight against the forces that oppress,
For in justice, there is the foundation for peace,
And in peace, the hope for a harmonious world.

2. Harmony is the fruit of justice,
To create a society where all can thrive,
Where conflict is resolved through understanding,
For harmony is not the absence of conflict,
But the presence of balance,
To nurture relationships that are strong,
To build communities that are united,
For in harmony, there is the essence of unity,
And in unity, the strength to endure.

3. Nurturing justice requires vigilance,
To be aware of the injustices that exist,
To not turn a blind eye,
For injustice thrives in silence,
To speak out, to take action,
To hold those in power accountable,
For in vigilance, there is protection,
And in protection, the power to preserve what is right.

4. Fostering harmony means embracing diversity,
To see the value in different perspectives,
To celebrate the richness of human experience,
For diversity is the strength of humanity,

To build a world where all are included,
Where all are valued,
For in diversity, there is beauty,
And in beauty, the foundation for a harmonious society.

5. Justice is the courage to challenge,
To confront the systems that oppress,
To fight against the forces of patriarchy,
To dismantle the structures of bigotry,
For justice is not complacent, but active,
To work for a world that is fair, that is just,
For in challenging power, there is liberation,
And in liberation, the creation of a just world.

6. Harmony is the art of compromise,
To find solutions that work for all,
To seek common ground,
For compromise is not weakness, but strength,
To listen, to understand, to negotiate,
To create a world where all are heard,
For in compromise, there is balance,
And in balance, the foundation for peace.

7. Nurturing justice means standing with the oppressed,
To be a voice for those who are silenced,
To fight for the rights of the marginalized,
For justice is the defense of the vulnerable,
To protect, to advocate, to empower,
For in standing with the oppressed, there is solidarity,
And in solidarity, the strength to fight for justice.

8. Fostering harmony requires empathy,
To feel the pain of others,
To understand the struggles of those different from us,
For empathy is the bridge to understanding,
To create a world where compassion rules,
Where kindness is the norm,
For in empathy, there is connection,

And in connection, the power to build harmony.

9. Justice is the pursuit of truth,
To uncover the lies that oppress,
To bring to light the truths that liberate,
For truth is the weapon of the just,
To expose, to reveal, to enlighten,
To create a world where truth prevails,
For in truth, there is power,
And in power, the foundation for a just society.

10. Harmony is the practice of respect,
To honor the dignity of each person,
To treat others as we wish to be treated,
For respect is the foundation of harmony,
To see the value in each individual,
To build relationships based on mutual regard,
For in respect, there is honor,
And in honor, the capacity to live in peace.

11. Nurturing justice is the commitment to equality,
To ensure that all have the same opportunities,
To fight against the disparities that divide,
For equality is the heart of justice,
To work for a world where all are equal,
Where no one is left behind,
For in equality, there is fairness,
And in fairness, the foundation for a just world.

12. Fostering harmony means healing the wounds of the past,
To acknowledge the wrongs that have been done,
To seek reconciliation, to seek forgiveness,
For healing is the path to harmony,
To mend the divides that separate us,
To move forward together,
For in healing, there is peace,
And in peace, the ability to build a united future.

13. Justice is the fight for liberation,
To free those who are bound by the chains of oppression,
To break the cycles of poverty, of inequality,
For liberation is the goal of justice,
To create a world where all are free,
Where all have the power to choose,
For in liberation, there is freedom,
And in freedom, the possibility of a just society.

14. Harmony is the pursuit of sustainability,
To live in balance with the earth,
To care for the environment, to protect our home,
For sustainability is the key to harmony,
To ensure that future generations inherit a world that is thriving,
To act with foresight, to act with care,
For in sustainability, there is the promise of a future,
And in the future, the potential for harmony.

15. Nurturing justice means embracing accountability,
To take responsibility for one's actions,
To hold others accountable for theirs,
For accountability is the foundation of trust,
To create a world where actions have consequences,
Where integrity is valued,
For in accountability, there is integrity,
And in integrity, the power to nurture a just world.

16. Justice requires the dismantling of oppression,
To break down the walls that confine,
To free those who are trapped in cycles of abuse,
For oppression is the enemy of justice,
To create systems that uplift, that support,
To ensure that power is used for good,
For in dismantling oppression, there is freedom,
And in freedom, the strength to build a just world.

17. Harmony is found in collaboration,

To work together towards common goals,
To pool our resources, our talents,
For collaboration is the heart of community,
To value each contribution, each effort,
To build a society where everyone has a role,
For in collaboration, there is unity,
And in unity, the foundation for peace.

18. Nurturing justice means advocating for the voiceless,
To speak for those who cannot speak for themselves,
To fight for those who are ignored,
For the voiceless are often the most oppressed,
To ensure that all voices are heard,
To create a world where everyone has a say,
For in advocacy, there is representation,
And in representation, the power to enact change.

19. Fostering harmony involves transparency,
To build trust through openness,
To ensure that actions are visible,
For transparency is the antidote to corruption,
To create systems that are honest, that are clear,
To ensure that justice is not just done, but seen to be done,
For in transparency, there is accountability,
And in accountability, the strength to foster harmony.

20. Justice is the fight against exploitation,
To protect the vulnerable from those who seek to profit,
To challenge the greed that drives inequality,
For exploitation is the root of injustice,
To ensure that all labor is valued,
That all people are treated fairly,
For in fighting exploitation, there is dignity,
And in dignity, the foundation for a just society.

21. Harmony is the celebration of community,
To find joy in coming together,
To celebrate the bonds that unite us,

For community is the fabric of society,
To build connections that are strong, that are lasting,
To create a world where no one is alone,
For in community, there is support,
And in support, the capacity to thrive.

22. Nurturing justice involves fair distribution,
To ensure that wealth is shared, not hoarded,
To fight against the concentration of power,
For inequality is the enemy of justice,
To create an economy that works for all,
Where resources are accessible, where opportunities are equal,
For in fair distribution, there is equity,
And in equity, the possibility of a balanced world.

23. Fostering harmony requires adaptability,
To be open to change, to growth,
To evolve as the world evolves,
For rigidity is the death of harmony,
To be flexible, to be open-minded,
To see change not as a threat, but as an opportunity,
For in adaptability, there is resilience,
And in resilience, the strength to maintain harmony.

24. Justice demands restitution,
To right the wrongs of the past,
To compensate those who have been harmed,
For restitution is the path to reconciliation,
To heal the wounds that have been inflicted,
To build a future that is fair, that is just,
For in restitution, there is justice,
And in justice, the power to create a new beginning.

25. Harmony is nurtured through understanding,
To seek to understand before seeking to be understood,
To learn from others, to share knowledge,
For understanding is the key to connection,
To build a world where knowledge is valued,

Where learning is a lifelong pursuit,
For in understanding, there is wisdom,
And in wisdom, the ability to foster harmony.

26. Nurturing justice involves courage,
To stand up against injustice,
To speak out when others remain silent,
For justice is not the path of least resistance,
To be brave, to be bold,
To fight for what is right, even when it is difficult,
For in courage, there is strength,
And in strength, the capacity to change the world.

27. Fostering harmony means promoting peace,
To work towards a world without war,
To resolve conflicts through dialogue,
For peace is the foundation of harmony,
To build relationships based on trust,
To create a world where violence is not the answer,
For in peace, there is security,
And in security, the foundation for a harmonious society.

28. Justice is found in equity,
To ensure that everyone has what they need,
To recognize that equality is not enough,
For equity is the true measure of fairness,
To provide resources, to provide support,
To create a society where everyone can succeed,
For in equity, there is justice,
And in justice, the foundation for a fair world.

Unremarkable 12, 2024

Book 11

1. Encouraging creativity begins with freedom,
To break the chains of conformity,
To explore beyond the boundaries set by others,
For creativity is the essence of the human spirit,
To imagine a world not as it is,
But as it could be,
For in creativity, there is liberation,
And in liberation, the potential for transformation.

2. Leading with heart means embracing vulnerability,
To show strength not through power,
But through authenticity,
For true leadership is not about domination,
But about connection, about care,
To lead by example, to lead with love,
For in vulnerability, there is trust,
And in trust, the foundation for change.

3. Creativity is the courage to be different,
To stand out in a world that rewards sameness,
To innovate, to create, to inspire,
For difference is not a flaw but a gift,
To celebrate the unique, the unconventional,
To see the beauty in the unexpected,
For in difference, there is diversity,
And in diversity, the strength to grow.

4. Leading with heart means putting people first,
To value the well-being of others,
Over profit, over power,
For a leader's role is to serve,
To uplift, to empower,

To create environments where all can thrive,
For in service, there is honor,
And in honor, the legacy of a leader.

5. Encouraging creativity requires a safe space,
To create an environment where all ideas are welcome,
Where innovation is nurtured,
For creativity cannot thrive in fear,
To foster a culture of openness,
Where mistakes are seen as opportunities,
For in safety, there is freedom,
And in freedom, the birth of new ideas.

6. Leading with heart is about humility,
To know that no one has all the answers,
To be open to learning, to listening,
For a true leader is a lifelong student,
To value the input of others,
To build a team that is diverse, that is strong,
For in humility, there is wisdom,
And in wisdom, the guidance to lead.

7. Creativity is the key to problem-solving,
To see challenges not as obstacles,
But as opportunities for innovation,
For creativity finds solutions where none seem possible,
To think outside the box, to reimagine,
To build a world that is better, that is brighter,
For in creativity, there is possibility,
And in possibility, the promise of progress.

8. Leading with heart means leading with integrity,
To act with honesty, with fairness,
To be a leader who is trustworthy,
For integrity is the cornerstone of leadership,
To do what is right, even when it is hard,
To lead with principles, with conviction,
For in integrity, there is strength,

And in strength, the power to inspire.

9. Encouraging creativity is about embracing failure,
To see failure not as an end,
But as a stepping stone to success,
For failure is a teacher, a guide,
To learn, to adapt, to improve,
To create a culture where failure is not feared,
For in failure, there is growth,
And in growth, the seeds of innovation.

10. Leading with heart means being empathetic,
To understand the needs of others,
To lead with compassion, with care,
For empathy is the heart of leadership,
To build relationships that are strong,
To lead a team that is cohesive, that is united,
For in empathy, there is connection,
And in connection, the power to lead.

11. Creativity is the spark that ignites change,
To challenge the old, to bring in the new,
To disrupt the status quo,
For creativity is the engine of progress,
To see the world not as static,
But as a canvas for imagination,
For in creativity, there is the power to change,
And in change, the potential to build a better world.

12. Leading with heart is about being inclusive,
To create a space where all voices are heard,
Where all perspectives are valued,
For inclusion is the key to unity,
To lead a team that is diverse,
To build a world where everyone belongs,
For in inclusion, there is harmony,
And in harmony, the strength to succeed.

13. Encouraging creativity is about taking risks,
To step into the unknown,
To explore uncharted territories,
For creativity thrives on adventure,
To be bold, to be daring,
To push the boundaries of what is possible,
For in risk, there is reward,
And in reward, the fruits of creativity.

14. Leading with heart means being courageous,
To stand up for what is right,
To lead with conviction, with courage,
For courage is the soul of leadership,
To face challenges head-on,
To lead in the face of adversity,
For in courage, there is resilience,
And in resilience, the power to overcome.

15. Creativity is the light that guides,
To illuminate the path forward,
To shine a light in the darkness,
For creativity is the beacon of hope,
To inspire, to uplift, to motivate,
To create a world that is full of possibility,
For in creativity, there is vision,
And in vision, the blueprint for a brighter future.

16. Creativity thrives in collaboration,
To bring together different minds,
To blend diverse talents,
For collaboration is the engine of innovation,
To build on each other's strengths,
To create something greater than the sum of its parts,
For in collaboration, there is synergy,
And in synergy, the power to innovate.

17. Leading with heart is about being present,
To give your full attention,

To listen, to engage,
For presence is the gift of leadership,
To be there in the moment,
To lead with mindfulness, with awareness,
For in presence, there is respect,
And in respect, the foundation for trust.

18. Encouraging creativity means challenging norms,
To not accept things as they are,
But to question, to explore,
For norms are the barriers to innovation,
To push the boundaries, to think differently,
To create a world where creativity is valued,
For in challenging norms, there is growth,
And in growth, the potential to transform.

19. Leading with heart is about empowering others,
To give people the tools they need,
To help them grow, to help them succeed,
For empowerment is the mark of a true leader,
To build others up, to support their journey,
To create a culture of empowerment,
For in empowering others, there is strength,
And in strength, the capacity to lead with heart.

20. Creativity is the ability to see connections,
To find links where others see none,
To bring together ideas from different fields,
For creativity is the art of synthesis,
To create new concepts, new solutions,
To innovate by seeing the bigger picture,
For in connections, there is insight,
And in insight, the seeds of creativity.

21. Leading with heart means showing gratitude,
To appreciate the efforts of others,
To acknowledge their contributions,
For gratitude is the soul of leadership,

To build a culture of recognition,
To lead with kindness, with thanks,
For in gratitude, there is fulfillment,
And in fulfillment, the power to inspire.

22. Encouraging creativity is about curiosity,
To have a thirst for knowledge,
To explore, to discover,
For curiosity is the catalyst of innovation,
To ask questions, to seek answers,
To never be satisfied with the status quo,
For in curiosity, there is discovery,
And in discovery, the potential to innovate.

23. Leading with heart is about being resilient,
To withstand the storms,
To remain steady in times of change,
For resilience is the backbone of leadership,
To keep moving forward, to keep the faith,
To lead with perseverance, with strength,
For in resilience, there is the power to endure,
And in enduring, the ability to lead with heart.

24. Creativity is the spirit of play,
To find joy in the process,
To experiment, to have fun,
For play is the freedom of creativity,
To explore without fear of failure,
To innovate with a sense of wonder,
For in play, there is joy,
And in joy, the inspiration to create.

25. Leading with heart means leading by example,
To be the change you wish to see,
To act with integrity, with purpose,
For example is the language of leadership,
To inspire through action,
To lead with conviction, with truth,

For in example, there is influence,
And in influence, the capacity to lead.

26. Encouraging creativity means valuing the arts,
To see art not just as entertainment,
But as a vital part of life,
For the arts are the expression of the human soul,
To support artists, to nurture creativity,
To build a world where the arts are celebrated,
For in the arts, there is expression,
And in expression, the essence of creativity.

27. Leading with heart is about authenticity,
To be true to oneself, to one's values,
To lead with sincerity, with honesty,
For authenticity is the core of leadership,
To be real, to be genuine,
To lead with transparency, with trust,
For in authenticity, there is respect,
And in respect, the strength to lead.

28. Creativity is the ability to adapt,
To change with the times,
To innovate in the face of new challenges,
For adaptation is the resilience of creativity,
To evolve, to grow, to thrive,
To create a world that is dynamic, that is alive,
For in adaptation, there is survival,
And in survival, the innovation to lead.

Unremarkable 13, 2024

Book 12

The Practice of Simplicity, The Power of Place

1. The practice of simplicity is the embrace of less,
To strip away the excess, the unnecessary,
To find joy in the essential,
For simplicity is the antidote to greed,
To live with what we need, not what we want,
To value quality over quantity,
For in simplicity, there is freedom,
And in freedom, the clarity to live authentically.

2. The power of place is in its ability to ground,
To root us in the present,
To connect us to the here and now,
For place is the anchor of existence,
To find stability in the world around us,
To be present in the spaces we inhabit,
For in place, there is stability,
And in stability, the strength to face life's storms.

3. The practice of simplicity is a form of resistance,
To reject the constant call for more,
To stand against the culture of excess,
For simplicity is a return to what matters,
To live with intention, with purpose,
To focus on the meaningful, the real,
For in simplicity, there is purpose,
And in purpose, the path to a fulfilled life.

4. The power of place is in its capacity to inspire,
To draw creativity from the environment,
To find beauty in the landscape,
For place shapes our thoughts, our dreams,
To see the world with fresh eyes,

To be moved by the spaces we occupy,
For in place, there is inspiration,
And in inspiration, the birth of new ideas.

5. The practice of simplicity is about contentment,
To be satisfied with enough,
To not always seek more,
For contentment is the heart of simplicity,
To find happiness in what we have,
To live a life that is rich in meaning,
For in contentment, there is peace,
And in peace, the power to live with grace.

6. The power of place is in its ability to connect,
To bring people together,
To build communities that are strong,
For place is the heart of connection,
To create spaces where relationships flourish,
To find unity in shared experiences,
For in place, there is community,
And in community, the strength to stand together.

7. The practice of simplicity is the pursuit of clarity,
To clear the mind of clutter,
To focus on what is important,
For clarity is found in simplicity,
To see life without the distractions,
To know what truly matters,
For in clarity, there is vision,
And in vision, the guidance to live with purpose.

8. The power of place is in its memory,
To hold the stories of the past,
To remember the lives that were lived,
For place is a repository of history,
To connect with the legacy of those who came before,
To honor the past in the present,
For in memory, there is wisdom,

And in wisdom, the understanding to shape the future.

9. The practice of simplicity is a form of liberation,
To free oneself from the chains of materialism,
To live a life that is light, that is free,
For simplicity is the path to freedom,
To be unburdened by possessions,
To find joy in the simple, the everyday,
For in liberation, there is joy,
And in joy, the fullness of life.

10. The power of place is its influence on identity,
To shape who we are,
To influence how we see the world,
For identity is forged in the places we inhabit,
To find ourselves in the spaces we love,
To be molded by the environment,
For in place, there is identity,
And in identity, the grounding of the self.

11. The practice of simplicity is about focus,
To not be distracted by the noise,
To concentrate on what truly matters,
For focus is the essence of simplicity,
To channel energy into the meaningful,
To live a life that is directed, that is purposeful,
For in focus, there is strength,
And in strength, the ability to achieve.

12. The power of place is in its capacity to nurture,
To provide the space to grow, to thrive,
To be a haven in times of need,
For place is a sanctuary, a refuge,
To find solace in the familiar,
To be supported by the environment,
For in nurturing, there is growth,
And in growth, the potential to flourish.

13. The practice of simplicity is an act of courage,
To stand against the tide of consumerism,
To live a life that is different, that is true,
For courage is needed to choose simplicity,
To be content in a world that always wants more,
To live with integrity, with authenticity,
For in courage, there is truth,
And in truth, the foundation for a meaningful life.

14. The power of place is in its resilience,
To endure through time,
To withstand the changes, the challenges,
For resilience is the strength of place,
To remain constant, to be a rock,
To provide continuity in a changing world,
For in resilience, there is stability,
And in stability, the power to endure.

15. The practice of simplicity is about balance,
To live a life that is harmonious,
To find equilibrium in all things,
For balance is the goal of simplicity,
To not be swayed by extremes,
To live in moderation, with care,
For in balance, there is harmony,
And in harmony, the peace to live with joy.

16. The practice of simplicity is a return to nature,
To find peace in the natural world,
To live in harmony with the earth,
For nature is the essence of simplicity,
To follow the rhythms of the seasons,
To respect the cycles of life,
For in nature, there is simplicity,
And in simplicity, the wisdom to live well.

17. The power of place is in its storytelling,
To be a canvas for human expression,

To hold the tales of those who pass through,
For place captures the essence of existence,
To echo the voices of the past,
To inspire the dreams of the future,
For in storytelling, there is connection,
And in connection, the continuity of life.

18. The practice of simplicity is the pursuit of peace,
To find calm in the chaos,
To cultivate a serene mind,
For peace is born in simplicity,
To be still, to be quiet,
To embrace the tranquility of the present,
For in peace, there is simplicity,
And in simplicity, the harmony of being.

19. The power of place is in its transformation,
To evolve with time,
To adapt to the needs of those it holds,
For transformation is the life of place,
To change while holding onto essence,
To grow without losing identity,
For in transformation, there is renewal,
And in renewal, the potential to flourish.

20. The practice of simplicity is a celebration of life,
To find joy in the small things,
To appreciate the everyday miracles,
For life is rich in its simplicity,
To see the beauty in the mundane,
To celebrate the ordinary,
For in celebration, there is simplicity,
And in simplicity, the joy of being alive.

21. The power of place is in its ability to shape us,
To influence our thoughts, our actions,
To be a mirror to our souls,
For place is the mold of character,

To reflect the values we hold,
To shape the people we become,
For in shaping, there is influence,
And in influence, the essence of identity.

22. The practice of simplicity is about mindfulness,
To be aware of each moment,
To live consciously, with intent,
For mindfulness is the practice of presence,
To engage fully with life,
To be present in each experience,
For in mindfulness, there is simplicity,
And in simplicity, the depth of life.

23. The power of place is in its diversity,
To host a multitude of lives,
To be a home to all,
For diversity is the strength of place,
To nurture different cultures, different voices,
To create a tapestry of existence,
For in diversity, there is vibrancy,
And in vibrancy, the richness of life.

24. The practice of simplicity is an embrace of the natural,
To reject the artificial, the superficial,
To live a life that is genuine, that is real,
For simplicity is found in authenticity,
To be true to oneself, to one's values,
To live in accordance with nature,
For in authenticity, there is simplicity,
And in simplicity, the truth of who we are.

25. The power of place is in its sacredness,
To be a space of reflection, of meditation,
To hold the spiritual and the material,
For sacredness is the heart of place,
To create spaces where the soul can rest,
To honor the spiritual in the everyday,

For in sacredness, there is peace,
And in peace, the sanctity of life.

26. The practice of simplicity is about gratitude,
To appreciate what we have,
To not always seek more,
For gratitude is the essence of contentment,
To be thankful for the small blessings,
To live a life that is rich in appreciation,
For in gratitude, there is simplicity,
And in simplicity, the abundance of life.

27. The power of place is in its capacity to hold memory,
To be a witness to the unfolding of time,
To remember the moments that matter,
For memory is the soul of place,
To hold onto the past while moving forward,
To be a keeper of stories, of lives lived,
For in memory, there is continuity,
And in continuity, the preservation of history.

28. The practice of simplicity is about living lightly,
To tread gently on the earth,
To leave a small footprint,
For simplicity is found in sustainability,
To respect the environment,
To live in harmony with the natural world,
For in living lightly, there is respect,
And in respect, the longevity of life.

Unremarkable 14, 2024

In Conclusion

Revisiting the Core Themes

As we come to the close of our journey together, it's important to take a moment to reflect on the central themes that have guided us through these pages. At the heart of *Stoic Principles Reimagined for Modern Challenges* lies a deep commitment to self-awareness, the courage to challenge societal norms, and the relentless pursuit of justice. These themes are not just philosophical musings; they are calls to action, urging us to transform ourselves and, by extension, the world around us.

Throughout this book, we have explored the importance of self-awareness as a foundation for personal growth and social change. To truly understand the world, we must first understand ourselves, our motivations, our biases, and our potential for both harm and good. Self-awareness requires us to look inward, to question our assumptions, and to be honest about our own shortcomings. It is through this process of introspection that we begin to break free from the chains of ignorance and unconscious bias that hold us back. But self-awareness is not an end in itself; it is a starting point. It compels us to take responsibility for our actions, to live with integrity, and to strive for continuous improvement. By becoming more self-aware, we lay the groundwork for living authentically, making choices that are aligned with our deepest values, and contributing positively to the world around us.

Another core theme of this book is the courage to challenge societal norms and the systems of power that perpetuate inequality, injustice, and oppression. Patriarchy, bigotry, and unchecked capitalism have long dictated the structure of our societies, shaping our beliefs, behaviors, and institutions. These forces seek to maintain control, to silence dissent, and to uphold the status quo. But we have the power to challenge these norms. We can question the rules that govern our lives, reject the narratives that seek to divide us, and dismantle the structures that oppress. Challenging power is not just a political act; it is a moral imperative. It is about standing up for what is right, even when it is difficult, even when it is dangerous. It is about being a voice for the voiceless, a champion for the marginalized, and a beacon of hope for those who have been cast aside.

Stoic Principles Reimagined for Modern Challenges is a vision of a just and equitable world, where everyone is treated with dignity, respect, and compassion. Justice is not simply about punishing wrongdoing; it is about creating conditions where all people can thrive. It is about ensuring that everyone has access to the resources, opportunities, and rights they need to live a full and meaningful life. Pursuing justice requires us to act. It calls us to advocate for those who are marginalized, to fight against discrimination, and to work towards a society where equality is not just a dream but a reality. Justice is not a passive state; it is an active pursuit, a constant striving to create a world that is fair and inclusive. It is about holding ourselves and others accountable, about speaking out against injustice, and about being willing to make sacrifices for the greater good.

Throughout our journey, we have seen the transformative power of empathy and compassion. These qualities allow us to connect with others, to understand their experiences, and to see the world through their eyes. Empathy breaks down the barriers that divide us, fostering a sense of shared humanity and common purpose. Compassion moves us to action. It is not enough to feel empathy; we must also act on it. We must show compassion in our daily interactions, in the choices we make, and in the causes we support. Compassion is a powerful force for good, one that can heal wounds, build bridges, and create lasting change. By cultivating empathy and compassion, we create a world where kindness is valued, where love is the guiding principle, and where justice is a reality for all.

Reflecting on Personal Growth

As we conclude this journey, it is important to reflect on the personal growth we have experienced. Personal growth is not a destination but a continuous process of self-discovery, transformation, and becoming. It is about evolving, learning, and moving closer to the person we aspire to be. Throughout this book, we have explored the themes of self-awareness, challenging norms, and living authentically, each of these serves as a catalyst for personal growth.

Personal growth begins with self-awareness. By turning inward and examining our thoughts, beliefs, and actions, we develop a deeper understanding of ourselves. Self-awareness requires us to ask difficult questions: What are my values? What drives me? What are my biases and blind spots? It challenges us to look honestly at who we are, to confront our fears and insecurities, and to embrace our strengths and weaknesses.

This process is not always comfortable. It can reveal truths about ourselves that we might prefer to ignore. But growth requires discomfort. It is through facing these truths that we begin to change. Self-awareness helps us recognize the patterns that hold us back, the beliefs that no longer serve us, and the habits that keep us stuck. By becoming more aware, we gain the power to make different choices, to break free from old ways of being, and to create new, healthier patterns. Personal growth is about embracing change and letting go of what no longer serves us. It is about releasing the past, forgiving ourselves and others, and moving forward with a renewed sense of purpose. Letting go is not about forgetting; it is about understanding that holding onto resentment, anger, or regret only keeps us trapped. By letting go, we free ourselves to live fully in the present and to embrace the opportunities that each new moment offers.

Change is a natural part of life, and resisting it only causes suffering. Personal growth requires us to be adaptable, to be open to new experiences, and to be willing to change our minds. It is about being flexible, about learning from our experiences, and about continuously evolving. Embracing change means being willing to step outside of our comfort zones, to take risks, and to face the unknown. It is through change that we grow, that we discover new parts of ourselves, and that we become who we are meant to be.

Personal growth also involves building resilience. Life is filled with challenges, setbacks, and disappointments. Resilience is the ability to bounce back, to learn from these experiences, and to keep moving forward. It is about finding strength in adversity, about seeing challenges as opportunities for growth, and about refusing to be defeated by circumstances. Resilience is not about being unbreakable; it is about being able to bend without breaking, about finding hope in the midst of struggle, and about having the courage to continue even when things are difficult. By cultivating resilience, we develop the strength to face life's challenges with grace, courage, and determination. Resilience is not something we are born with; it is something we develop through experience, through reflection, and through a commitment to growth.

Personal growth is ultimately about living authentically. It is about being true to oneself, about expressing one's truth, and about living in alignment with one's values. Authenticity requires us to let go of the need for approval, to stop comparing ourselves to others, and to trust in our own path. It is about embracing our uniqueness, celebrating our individuality, and being confident in who we are. Living authentically means making choices that reflect our true selves, that honor our values, and that contribute to our well-being and the well-being of others. It is about being honest, transparent, and genuine. By living authentically, we create a life that is meaningful, fulfilling, and aligned with our highest aspirations. Authenticity is the foundation of personal growth, and through it, we find the freedom to be who we truly are.

Reflecting on personal growth is an opportunity to acknowledge how far we have come, to celebrate our progress, and to set our intentions for the future. Personal growth is not a linear path; it is a journey with twists and turns, ups and downs, but it is a journey worth taking. By embracing self-awareness, change, resilience, and authenticity, we continue to grow, to evolve, and to become the best version of ourselves. Personal growth is a lifelong journey, and with each step, we move closer to the person we are meant to be.

The Role of Community

Throughout our journey of personal growth and social transformation, one truth stands out: we are not alone. The power of community is immense. It is in community that we find support, connection, and the strength to continue when the road is hard. Community is about more than just being together; it is about belonging, about finding a place where we are accepted, valued, and understood.

Community offers us a sense of connection that is fundamental to our well-being. In a world that often emphasizes individualism and competition, community reminds us that we are part of something larger than ourselves. It teaches us that our actions have an impact on others and that we are interconnected. Through community, we learn empathy, compassion, and cooperation. We see firsthand how we can support each other, lift each other up, and create positive change together. Being part of a community provides us with a network of support. When we face challenges, it is our community that helps us through. It is the friends, family, and allies who stand by us, who offer a listening ear, a helping hand, and a sense of solidarity. This support is not just emotional; it is practical. It is in community that we find the resources, knowledge, and skills we need to navigate life's challenges. By being part of a community, we are stronger, more resilient, and better equipped to face whatever comes our way.

Creating and sustaining communities requires effort, intention, and commitment. It is not just about coming together; it is about building relationships based on trust, respect, and shared values. A true community is one where everyone feels heard, where every voice is valued, and where differences are celebrated. It is a space where we can be our authentic selves, without fear of judgment or exclusion. To build such communities, we must be willing to invest time and energy into our relationships. We must listen, communicate, and be open to

144

understanding others' perspectives. Building community means creating spaces where people feel safe, welcome, and supported. It means being inclusive, ensuring that everyone has a seat at the table, and that no one is left behind. Sustaining community also means being willing to address conflicts, to have difficult conversations, and to work through differences. It requires patience, empathy, and a commitment to finding common ground. Community is not about avoiding conflict; it is about handling it constructively, about finding solutions that respect everyone's needs and perspectives.

Communities are not just places of support; they are powerful catalysts for change. When people come together with a shared purpose, they can achieve incredible things. Community action has the power to challenge injustice, to advocate for rights, and to create a better world. It is through community that movements are born, that voices are amplified, and that change is realized. Communities have the power to hold those in power accountable, to demand transparency, and to fight for justice. They can challenge the status quo, push for policy changes, and create new systems that are fair and equitable. By working together, communities can make a real difference, both locally and globally. The role of community is central to our growth, our well-being, and our ability to create change. It is in community that we find the support we need, the connections that sustain us, and the power to make a difference.

The Impact of Challenging Power

Challenging power is a bold act, one that requires courage, conviction, and a commitment to justice. Throughout history, power has been used to control, to silence, and to oppress. Whether it is political, economic, or social, power concentrated in the hands of a few often leads to the marginalization of many. But when we challenge power, we disrupt this cycle. We create the possibility for change, for justice, and for a society where power is shared equitably.

The first impact of challenging power is that it exposes injustice. Systems of power thrive in darkness, where secrecy and control keep their true nature hidden. By questioning authority, by shining a light on corruption, and by speaking truth to power, we reveal the injustices that are often hidden from view. This exposure is the first step towards change. When injustice is brought to light, it can no longer be ignored. People become aware, they start to ask questions, and they begin to demand answers. Challenging power forces us to confront uncomfortable truths about our society. It reveals the ways in which power is used to maintain inequality, to exploit resources, and to prioritize profit over people. By challenging power, we challenge the narrative that says, "This is just the way things are." We question the systems that uphold inequality, and we push for a new narrative, one that values fairness, justice, and the well-being of all.

Another significant impact of challenging power is the empowerment of marginalized communities. Power dynamics are often designed to silence those who are most affected by injustice. When we challenge power, we amplify the voices of those who have been silenced. We create space for marginalized communities to speak out, to be heard, and to lead. Empowerment is about more than just giving people a voice; it is about supporting them in reclaiming their power, in demanding their rights, and in shaping their own futures.

146

Challenging power shifts the balance. It disrupts the status quo and opens up opportunities for those who have been excluded. It allows for new perspectives, new ideas, and new leaders to emerge. By challenging power, we not only fight against oppression, but we also build a foundation for a more inclusive and equitable society.

Challenging power is not just about opposition; it is about creating pathways for change. It is about identifying the flaws in the system and proposing solutions. It is about advocating for policies that promote justice, equity, and sustainability. By challenging power, we push for reforms that benefit the many, not just the few. We create the conditions for real, lasting change. Change does not happen overnight. It requires persistence, dedication, and a clear vision of what we want to achieve. By challenging power, we set the stage for these changes to occur. We create momentum, we build movements, and we inspire others to join us. Challenging power is not a solitary act; it is a collective effort, one that requires the participation and support of many. Together, we have the power to transform our society, to dismantle systems of oppression, and to create a world that is just, compassionate, and fair.

The Importance of Courage and Action

Courage is the driving force behind every meaningful change. It is the inner strength that propels us to act in the face of fear, uncertainty, and opposition. Courage is not the absence of fear; rather, it is the decision to move forward despite it. Throughout history, every movement for justice, equality, and freedom has been fueled by the courage of individuals who dared to challenge the status quo, who refused to accept the world as it was, and who took action to create the world as it should be.

Courage is the spark that ignites change. It begins with the courage to question, to challenge, and to speak out. It requires us to confront uncomfortable truths, to stand up against injustice, and to advocate for those who are silenced. Courage drives us to take risks, to push beyond our comfort zones, and to make sacrifices for the greater good. It is through courageous acts that we disrupt systems of oppression, challenge entrenched power, and create opportunities for progress. Without courage, there can be no change. It is easy to remain passive, to be complacent, and to accept things as they are. But change demands action, and action requires courage. It is the courage to stand alone, to face criticism, and to persevere that brings about real, lasting change. Every step towards justice, every victory for equality, begins with an act of courage. Courage must be paired with action. It is not enough to feel strongly about injustice; we must also be willing to act. Action is what turns our beliefs into reality, our values into practice, and our vision into existence. Acting means making choices that align with our principles, advocating for change, and being an active participant in the creation of a better world.

Fostering Empathy and Compassion

In a world that often feels divided and disconnected, empathy and compassion are powerful tools for healing and transformation. They are the bridges that connect us to one another, allowing us to see beyond our own experiences and understand the lives of others. Empathy and compassion are not just emotions; they are practices, ways of being that require us to open our hearts and minds. They challenge us to be present with others, to listen deeply, and to respond with kindness.

Empathy is the ability to understand and share the feelings of another. It allows us to put ourselves in someone else's shoes, to see the world through their eyes, and to feel what they feel. Empathy breaks down the barriers that divide us, race, gender, class, and more, and reveals our shared humanity. It reminds us that, despite our differences, we are all connected by the common experiences of joy, pain, hope, and struggle. Empathy is not a passive quality; it is an active engagement with the lives of others. It requires us to listen without judgment, to be present without distraction, and to offer support without expectation. By practicing empathy, we create a space where people feel seen, heard, and valued. We build relationships based on understanding and trust, and we foster a culture of respect and inclusion. Empathy is a catalyst for compassion, and it is through empathy that we begin to care for others as we care for ourselves.

While empathy allows us to feel with others, compassion moves us to act on their behalf. Compassion is empathy in action; it is the desire to alleviate suffering and to bring comfort and support to those in need. Compassion is not pity; it is a deep, genuine concern for the well-being of others. It is about recognizing the inherent worth of every person and treating them with kindness, dignity, and respect. Compassion requires us to go beyond our own self-interest, to consider the needs of others, and to take action to support them. It might mean offering a listening ear, providing practical help, or standing up for those who are marginalized and oppressed. Compassion is a powerful force for change, one that has the ability to transform not only individual lives but entire communities. By fostering compassion, we create a world where love, kindness, and care are the guiding principles.

Fostering empathy and compassion is a practice that begins with small, everyday actions. It starts with being present, with paying attention to the people around us, and with listening deeply to their stories. It means being curious about others, asking questions, and being open to understanding different perspectives. It requires us to be patient, to give others the time and space to express themselves, and to respond with kindness. Cultivating empathy and compassion also means being kind to ourselves. We cannot give what we do not have, and self-compassion is the foundation of compassion for others. By treating ourselves with kindness, forgiveness, and care, we build the capacity to extend those same qualities to others. Empathy and compassion remind us of our shared humanity, they inspire us to care for one another, and they move us to act in ways that uplift and support. By fostering empathy and compassion, we create a ripple effect of kindness and understanding that reaches far beyond ourselves. In a world that can sometimes feel harsh and divided, empathy and compassion are the lights that guide us towards connection, healing, and peace.

Embracing Creativity and Innovation

Creativity and innovation are the lifeblood of progress. They are the forces that propel us beyond the ordinary, that inspire us to imagine new possibilities, and that enable us to solve the complex challenges we face. In a world where conformity often reigns, embracing creativity and innovation is an act of courage. It is about thinking differently, challenging the status quo, and daring to envision a future that is better than the present.

Creativity is not just about art or self-expression; it is a way of approaching the world. It involves seeing beyond what is, to what could be. Creative thinking allows us to break free from the limitations of conventional wisdom and to explore new ideas, perspectives, and solutions. It is through creativity that we find new ways to address old problems, to challenge outdated systems, and to create innovative paths forward. By embracing creativity, we open ourselves up to a world of possibilities. We allow ourselves to dream, to experiment, and to play. Creativity encourages us to take risks, to learn from failure, and to keep trying until we find a way that works. It is a process of discovery, one that requires us to be curious, open-minded, and willing to explore the unknown. Through creative thinking, we become innovators, problem-solvers, and visionaries.

Innovation is the application of creativity to real-world challenges. It is about turning ideas into action, about finding practical solutions to pressing problems, and about creating new opportunities for growth and development. Innovation is not just about technology or business; it is about creating positive change in every aspect of life, social, economic, environmental, and beyond. In a rapidly changing world, innovation is essential. It allows us to adapt to new realities, to respond to emerging needs, and to build a future that is sustainable, just, and inclusive. Innovation challenges us to think outside the box, to question the status quo, and to be willing to disrupt systems that no longer serve us. It is through innovation that we find new ways to live, work, and thrive together.

To embrace creativity and innovation, we must create environments that encourage and support these qualities. This means fostering a culture where new ideas are welcomed, where experimentation is encouraged, and where failure is seen as a stepping stone to success. It means creating spaces where people feel safe to express their ideas, to challenge assumptions, and to collaborate with others. Cultivating a culture of creativity and innovation requires us to be open-minded, flexible, and adaptable. It requires us to value diversity, to recognize that different perspectives bring new insights, and to celebrate the unique contributions of each individual. It means being willing to listen, to learn, and to grow.

Innovation often involves venturing into the unknown, and this can be uncomfortable. It requires us to let go of the need for certainty, to embrace ambiguity, and to be willing to take risks. But it is in the unknown that new possibilities are born. By embracing the unknown, we open ourselves up to new experiences, new ideas, and new ways of being. Creativity and innovation are not just about what we do; they are about how we think, how we see the world, and how we engage with it. By embracing creativity and innovation, we become agents of change, capable of transforming our lives and the world around us. We become leaders, visionaries, and pioneers, blazing new trails and creating a future that reflects our highest aspirations.

Building a Vision for the Future

Building a vision for the future is about more than imagining what could be, it's about creating a roadmap for what will be. A vision gives us direction, purpose, and motivation. It serves as a beacon of hope, guiding us through challenges and inspiring us to keep moving forward. A meaningful vision is rooted in our values and our dreams for a better world. It reflects our commitment to justice, equality, and compassion. To build a vision for the future, we must start by asking ourselves: What kind of world do we want to live in? What values do we want to uphold? How can we contribute to making that vision a reality? A vision for the future is one that is inclusive, where every person is treated with dignity and respect, where resources are shared equitably, and where the environment is protected for future generations. It is a world where power is used responsibly, where differences are celebrated, and where everyone has the opportunity to thrive.

Creating this vision requires imagination, courage, and a willingness to think beyond the limitations of the present. It means envisioning new possibilities, challenging the status quo, and daring to dream big. Our vision for the future should inspire us, motivate us, and remind us of what we are working towards. By holding this vision close, we keep our purpose clear, our actions focused, and our spirits strong.

Turning our vision into reality requires action. Here are some practical steps for moving forward:

1. Educate Yourself and Others: Knowledge is power. Take the time to learn about the issues that matter most to you, social justice, environmental sustainability, economic inequality, and more. Share what you learn with others. Education is a powerful tool for raising awareness, building understanding, and inspiring action.

2. Get Involved in Your Community: Change starts at the local level. Get involved in your community, join local organizations, attend town hall meetings, volunteer for causes you care about. By engaging with your community, you build connections, learn from others, and make a direct impact.

3. Advocate for Change: Use your voice to advocate for policies and practices that align with your vision. Write letters to your representatives, participate in protests, sign petitions, and support advocacy groups. Advocacy is about speaking up for what you believe in and pushing for systemic change.

4. Practice Empathy and Compassion: Building a better future requires us to care for one another. Practice empathy and compassion in your daily life. Listen to others, offer support, and show kindness. Small acts of compassion can have a big impact, creating ripples of positivity and connection.

5. Live Your Values: Align your actions with your values. Make choices that reflect your commitment to justice, equality, and sustainability. Whether it's how you spend your money, how you interact with others, or how you use your time, make decisions that support your vision for the future.

6. Collaborate and Build Alliances: We are stronger together. Collaborate with others who share your vision and goals. Build alliances, form partnerships, and work together to create change. Collective action amplifies our impact and brings us closer to our shared vision.

As we come to the end of this journey, I leave you with a final call to supportive action. The world we envision, a world of justice, compassion, and equality, requires each of us to play our part. Change does not happen in isolation; it happens when individuals come together, united by a common purpose and a shared commitment to making a difference. Let us not be content with the way things are. Let us not be silent in the face of injustice or passive in the face of suffering. Instead, let us be active participants in the creation of a better world. Let us challenge the systems that oppress, advocate for those who are marginalized, and stand up for what is right.

Supportive action means being there for one another. It means lifting each other up, offering a helping hand, and working together towards our common goals. It means being allies, being advocates, and being agents of change. The challenges we face are great, but so is our potential to overcome them. Together, we have the power to transform our society, to build a future that reflects our highest ideals, and to create a world where everyone can thrive. This is our moment. Let us rise to it with courage, with compassion, and with a commitment to action. Let us be the change we wish to see, knowing that each of us has a role to play, a voice to share, and a difference to make. The future is ours to create, and with supportive action, we can make it a reality.

Unremarkable 15, 2024

Thank You Marcus Aurelius

Meditations for a New Era

As we conclude this reimagined journey through Meditations, it is clear that the wisdom of Marcus Aurelius has transcended time. His reflections, born from the challenges of his era, remain profoundly relevant today. Yet, as with all timeless works, the interpretations and applications must evolve to resonate with the present. In *Stoic Principles Reimagined for Modern Challenges*, we have taken the ancient wisdom of Aurelius and infused it with the urgent themes of our time: anti-patriarchy, anti-bigotry, and anti-capitalism. This reimagining is not about rewriting the past but about bringing the wisdom of the past into dialogue with the issues of today.

Our world today faces complex challenges, inequality, injustice, environmental degradation, and widespread division. In such a landscape, the stoic principles of self-awareness, resilience, and compassion are more crucial than ever. These principles provide us with the tools to navigate our personal lives with integrity and to engage with the world in meaningful ways. *Stoic Principles Reimagined for Modern Challenges* calls on us to use these tools to challenge the systemic injustices that persist and to actively participate in building a better world. Marcus Aurelius taught us to reflect on our own nature, to understand our role in the broader cosmos, and to live in accordance with virtue. In our reimagining, these reflections take on new dimensions. They compel us to question not only our personal actions but also the societal structures that shape our lives. They invite us to challenge power imbalances, to stand up against discrimination, and to create systems that are fair and just for all.

The reimagined meditations remind us that our growth and fulfillment are intertwined with the well-being of others. In a globalized world, our actions ripple across communities, societies, and the planet. We have a collective responsibility to act with empathy and compassion, to uplift those who are marginalized, and to protect the environment for future generations. Marcus Aurelius spoke of the interconnectedness of all things; today, this interconnectedness means recognizing our impact on each other and the world.

This modern interpretation of Meditations challenges us to look beyond our own comfort and to engage with the pressing issues of our time. It calls us to be allies in the fight against racism, sexism, and economic inequality. It calls us to be stewards of the earth, advocating for sustainable practices and protecting the natural world. It calls us to be voices for justice, ensuring that all people have the opportunity to thrive.

While this reimagined work seeks to address contemporary issues, it is deeply indebted to the original Meditations of Marcus Aurelius. His writings offer a profound exploration of human nature, the pursuit of virtue, and the importance of living in harmony with oneself and the world. Marcus Aurelius's reflections on the impermanence of life, the power of the mind, and the importance of moral integrity are timeless truths that continue to guide us. We owe a great debt to Marcus Aurelius for his insights into the human condition. His stoic philosophy has provided a framework for understanding the challenges we face, both personal and societal. It has taught us the value of resilience in the face of adversity, the importance of inner peace amidst chaos, and the need for continuous self-improvement. These lessons are as relevant now as they were two millennia ago.

As we move forward with the lessons from *Stoic Principles Reimagined for Modern Challenges*, let us carry with us the spirit of both reflection and action. Reflection helps us understand our own minds, to cultivate self-awareness and empathy. Action compels us to take what we have learned and apply it to the world around us. The true power of these meditations lies in their ability to transform our thoughts into deeds, to turn our intentions into reality. Let us be guided by the principles of justice, compassion, and integrity. Let us strive to live authentically, to challenge the norms that no longer serve us, and to build a future that reflects our highest values. The wisdom of Marcus Aurelius reminds us that we are all part of a larger whole, and our actions have the power to shape the world. By embracing these reimagined meditations, we take a step towards creating a world that is more just, more compassionate, and more aligned with the values we hold dear.

As we draw this moment closed, let us remember that the journey of self-discovery and social transformation is ongoing. *Stoic Principles Reimagined for Modern Challenges* is not an end but a beginning, an invitation to reflect deeply, to live with intention, and to act with purpose. The challenges we face are great, but so is our capacity to meet them with courage, wisdom, and compassion. In honoring the legacy of Marcus Aurelius, let us also honor the legacy we wish to leave. Let us be the generation that rises to the challenge, that embraces the power of thought and action, and that builds a future worthy of our highest aspirations. The meditations of Marcus Aurelius have guided us this far; now it is up to us to carry them forward, to reimagine them for our time, and to use them as a compass for the journey ahead.

The future is ours to shape, and with the wisdom of the past and the vision of the present, we have the power to create a world that reflects the best of who we are and the best of what we can be. Let us go forth with the knowledge that our reflections matter, our actions matter, and together, we can create a world that is just, compassionate, and filled with possibility.

List of Prints

About the author

The author lives removed.

Please feel free to burn part or all of this book, safely, as an effigy.

www.ingramcontent.com/pod-product-compliance
Lightning Source LLC
Chambersburg PA
CBHW020934090426
42736CB00010B/1135